Publisher: Military History Group, London, United Kingdom.

E-Mail: milhisgroup@gmail.com

Print: Lulu Press, Inc., Lulu Press, Inc. 627 Davis Drive Suite 300 Morrisville, NC 27560, USA. Massachusetts, US; Wisconsin, US; Ontario, Canada; Île-de-France, France; Wielkopolska, Poland; Cambridgeshire, United Kingdom; Victoria, Australia.

Text © 2020, 2023 Bernhard Kast and Christoph Bergs. All Rights reserved.

Cover design by M. Koskela.

Illustrations by Bernhard Kast.

Corrected & Expanded Edition.

Any total or partial reproduction, copying, representation, adaptation, modification, or transfer of this book, its content or visuals, whether for commercial or non-commercial purposes, is forbidden without express, prior and written consent by the authors.
Quotations of the book with proper citation (authors, title, page number) are of course allowed.

ISBN 978-1-915453-16-7

> Dies ist ein geheimer Gegenstand im Sinne des § 88 Reichsstrafgesetzbuchs (Fassung vom 24. April 1934). Mißbrauch wird nach den Bestimmungen dieses Gesetzes bestraft, sofern nicht andere Strafbestimmungen in Frage kommen.

[Dieser Text wurde im Original auf der Rückseite des Buchumschlages gedruckt.]

> This is a secret publication subject to § 88 Reich Penal Code (version of 24 April 1934). Misuse shall be punished in accordance to the provisions of this law, unless other penal provisions apply.

[This text was printed on the reverse of the front cover in the original.]

Einführung – Zuerst lesen

Um eine authentische Repräsentation einer Heeresdruckvorschift[1] in englischer Sprache zu präsentieren, hält sich diese Übersetzung so nahe wie möglich am Originaltext. Dadurch entstanden im Lauf der Zeit einige Probleme, denn Wortkonstruktionen und Redewendungen aus dem „militärischen Deutsch" der 40er Jahre lassen sich in manchen Fällen nicht eins zu eins ins Englische übertragen. Die Übersetzung historischer Dokumente ist naturgemäß eine ungenaue Disziplin, irreführende oder unklare Formulierungen in der Übersetzung sind daher nicht auszuschließen.

Dies lässt sich anhand der Wörter „Entfaltung" und „Entwicklung" gut darstellen. Eine direkte Übersetzung in „unfolding" und „development" würde nur beschränkt die Originalbedeutung widerspiegeln. Außerdem gab es auf Grund von Bedeutungswandel über die Jahre hinweg auch noch eine Änderung des US-Amerikanischen Äquivalents. Im Glossar finden sich vertiefende Anmerkungen hierzu.

Dadurch ist es möglich, dass die englische Übersetzung Interpretationsspielraum lässt, der im Originalkontext nicht gegeben ist. Für solche Fälle wurden, z.T. auch für das deutsche Original, erklärende Fußnoten hinzugefügt. Die im Originaltext abgedruckten Fußnoten befinden sich ihrer originalen Formatierung direkt unter dem Text und sind an Hand einer hochgestellten Ziffer gefolgt von einer geschlossenen Klammer, z. B.: ¹) zu identifizieren. Die von uns hinzugefügten Fußnoten befinden sich in der gängigen Position unterhalb der Seite. Zum besseren Verständnis des Fließtexts wurden nötige Ergänzungen in eckigen Klammern „[ ]" eingefügt.

Die Formatierung folgt ebenfalls soweit möglich dem Originaltext. Es wurde lediglich zwecks einfacherer Lesbarkeit gesperrter T e x t durch kursiven *Text* ersetzt. Da der Originaltext aus 1941 stammt, finden sich vereinzelt Wörter, die nach der heutigen Rechtschreibungsnorm anders geschrieben werden. Bedingt durch die Originalformatierungen finden sich auch vereinzelt leere Passagen und Seiten im Text wieder.

Abschließend sei vermerkt, dass das Wort „Panzerkampfwagen" mit „tank" übersetzt wurde. Davon ausgenommen sind jene Passagen in denen auf einen speziellen Panzertyp verwiesen wird, z.B.: „Panzerkampfwagen IV", um so die klare Unterscheidung wie im Originaltext zu belassen.

Wir wünschen Ihnen viel Spaß mit dieser Übersetzung einer Heeresdruckvorschrift aus dem Jahre 1941.

Bernhard Kast
Christoph Bergs

---

[1] Wehrmacht ungleich Bundeswehr, dort bedeutet "H. Dv." Heeresdienstvorschrift.

Introduction – Read First

In order to publish an authentic representation of a German Army Regulation[2] in English, this translation remains as close to the original text as possible. This presented certain problems, because German composite words and phrases used in "military German" from the 1940s often cannot be translated word-for-word into English. The translation of historic documents is not an exact discipline, as such we cannot rule out misleading or unclear phrases in the translation.

The German words "Entfaltung" and "Entwicklung" demonstrate this well, as a direct translation into "unfolding" and "development" would only partially reflect the original meaning. Additionally, due to semantic changes over the years there was also a change of the US-American equivalent. Further information on this case can be found in the Glossary.

Therefore, it is possible that the English translations leave some room for interpretation that is not given in the original document. To clarify such passages for the reader, we provided footnotes when needed. The original footnotes were retained together with their original formatting and can be found directly below the text, identifiable by a superscript number followed by a closing parenthesis, e.g., [1]). Additional footnotes added by us can be found in the usual position at the bottom of the page. To facilitate comprehension, additions to the text have been made within brackets "[ ]".

The formatting remains wherever possible based on the original text. Only spaced t e x t was replaced with italic *text* for reasons of legibility. Since the original text is from 1941 the spelling of some German words might also differ from today's spelling norms. Due to the original page formatting, some empty space or even empty pages can occasionally be found.

As a final note, it should be mentioned that the word "Panzerkampfwagen" has been translated with "tank". This applies to all cases except when the original refers to a specific type of tank, e.g., "Panzerkampfwagen IV". This was kept in our translation to provide the same clear distinction as in the original.

We hope you enjoy this translated version of a German Army Regulation from 1941.

Bernhard Kast
Christoph Bergs

---

[2] The literal translation of a Heeresdruckvorschrift would be "Army Print Regulation". In the Bundeswehr the abbreviation "H. Dv." stands for "Army Service Regulation".

Danksagung

Während wir an diesem Projekt gearbeitet haben, haben uns verschiedene Menschen mit konstruktiven Hinweisen und Kritik geholfen damit diese Publikation gemacht werden konnte. An dieser Stelle möchten wir besonders danken: Nicholas „the Chieftain" Moran, Dr. Roman Töppel, Jens Wehner, Many Miles Away und Navaronegun.

Wir möchten außerdem einen besonderen Dank an unsere Unterstützer auf Patreon, PayPal und Subscribestar aussprechen, als auch unseren Discord Mitgliedern und die größere Community für die kontinuierliche Unterstützung. Ohne diese hätte dieses Projekt niemals das Licht der Welt erblickt. Zusätzlich gab es einige wenige Unterstützter, die uns im außerordentlichen Maße materiell unterstützt haben, diese sind:

Andrew Gianelli (US)

Stefan Jovanovich (US)

Jack Ray (US)

Producers

Besonderer Dank gilt den folgenden fünf Producern, die diese Publikation möglich gemacht haben:

Martin Nyberg

Jack Ray

Gustav Erik Åberg

Conrad Deenen

Lucas Baptista Martins

Acknowledgements

Throughout our work on this project, various individuals have provided constructive insights and criticism that have helped us in making this publication. At this point, we would like to thank them and specifically: Nicholas "the Chieftain" Moran, Dr. Roman Töppel, Jens Wehner, Many Miles Away and Navaronegun.

We would also like to extend a special thanks to our Patreon, PayPal and Subscribestar supporters, as well as our Discord crews and wider community for supporting our continuous endeavors. Without them, this project would never have seen the light of day. Additionally, there were a few selected supporters, who went above and beyond the call of duty and provided substantial material support to us over the years, these are:

Andrew Gianelli (US)

Stefan Jovanovich (US)

Jack Ray (US)

Producers

Special thanks to the following five Producers, who made this publication possible:

Martin Nyberg

Jack Ray

Gustav Erik Åberg

Conrad Deenen

Lucas Baptista Martins

H. Dv. 470/7

<u>Nur für den Dienstgebrauch!</u>

Ausbildungsvorschrift für die Panzertruppe
(A. B. Pz.)

Heft 7
Die mittlere Panzerkompanie

Vom 1. 5. 41

Berlin 1941
Gedruckt in der Reichsdruckerei

H. Dv. 470/7

<u>For Official Use Only!</u>

Training Regulations For The Armored Troops (A. B. Pz.)

Issue 7
The Medium Tank Company

From 1. 5. 41[1]

Berlin 1941
Printed in the Reich Printing Press

---

[1] Day, Month, Year, so 1st May 1941.

Der Oberbefehlshaber
des Heeres   H. Qu. O. K. H.[2], 1. 5. 41
Gen. St. d. H. / Gen. d. Schn. Tr.[3]
  b. Ob. d. H.[4]

Ich genehmige die „Ausbildungsvorschrift für die Panzertruppe (A. B. Pz.) Heft 7"

„Die mittlere Panzerkompanie".

Mit dem Erscheinen dieser Vorschrift tritt der Vorabdruck H. Dv. 470/3b, „Die mittlere Panzerkompanie" vom 11. 10. 1939 außer Kraft.

von Brauchitsch[5]

---

[2] Hauptquartier Oberkommando des Heeres (OKH).

[3] Generalstab des Heeres / General der Schnellen Truppen. Die „Schnelle Truppe" war der Vorläufer der „Panzertruppe" (ab April 1943), sie umfasste Panzereinheiten, Panzerabwehreinheiten, motorisierte Schützeneinheiten, motorisierte Kavallerieeinheiten, Reiter- und Radfahreinheiten, Panzeraufklärungseinheiten und motorisierte Aufklärungseinheiten. Allerdings waren zum Beispiel Panzerabwehreinheiten, die Teil der Grenadierregimenter waren nicht Teil der „Panzertruppe"/"Schnellen Truppe".

[4] beim Oberbefehlshaber des Heeres.

[5] Generalfeldmarschall Walther von Brauchitsch (1881-1948), Oberbefehlshaber des Heers (1938-1941).

The Commander-in-Chief
of the Army H. Qu. O. K.H.[6], 1. 5. 41
Gen. St. d. H. / Gen. d. Schn. Tr.[7]
b. Ob. d. H.[8]

I approve the "Training Regulations for the Armored Troops (A. B. Pz.) Issue 7".

"The Medium Tank Company."

With the appearance of this regulation the preprint H. Dv. 470/3b, "The Medium Tank Company" of 11. 10. 1939 expires.

von Brauchitsch[9]

---

[6] Army High Command Headquarters.

[7] General Staff of the Army / General of the Mobile Troops. The "Mobile Troops" (literally "Fast Troops") was the forerunner of the "Armored Troops" (from April 1943), which comprised tank units, anti-tank units, motorized infantry units, motorized cavalry units, cavalry and bicycle units, tank reconnaissance units and motorized reconnaissance units. However, for example, anti-tank defense units that were part of the Grenadier regiments were not part of the "Armored Troops"/"Mobile Troops".

[8] with the Commander-in-Chief of the Army.

[9] Field Marshal Walther von Brauchitsch (1881-1948), Commander-in-Chief of the Army (1938-1941).

Inhaltsverzeichnis

	Seite
A. Wesen und Gliederung der mittleren Panzerkompanie	5
B. Ausbildung	7
I. Leitsätze für Erziehung und Ausbildung. Ausbildungsziele	7
II. Ausbildung am Panzerkampfwagen	9
III. Sonderausbildung	11
C. Der einzelne Panzerkampfwagen	13
D. Der Zug	18
Allgemeines	18
a) Der mittlere Panzerkampfwagenzug	19
1. Formen und Bewegungen	19
2. Der mittlere Zug im Gefecht	28
b) Der leichte Zug	33
1. Formen und Bewegungen	35
2. Der leichte Zug im Gefecht	44
E. Die Kompanie	47
I. Allgemeines	47
II. Formen und Bewegungen	49
III. Führung	57
IV. Marsch und Gefecht	58
a) Marsch	58
b) Entfaltung	60

Table of Contents

	Page
A. Nature and Composition of the Medium Tank Company	5
B. Education and Training	7
I. Guidelines for Education and Training. Educational Goals	7
II. Training on a Tank	9
III. Special Training	11
C. The Individual Tank	13
D. The Platoon	18
General Information	18
a) The Medium Tank Platoon	19
1. Formations and Movements	19
2. The Medium Platoon in an Engagement	28
b) The Light Platoon	33
1. Formation and Movements	35
2. The Light Platoon in an Engagement	44
E. The Company	47
I. General Information	47
II. Formations and Movements	49
III. Command	57
IV. March and Engagement	58
a) March	58
b) Preliminary Deployment[10]	60

---

[10] See in Supplement 2: Section "A Note about the Use of 'Deployment' [...] ".

	Seite
c) Angriff	60
Angriff aus der Bewegung	63
Angriff aus der Bereitstellung	64
d) Kampf unter besonderen Verhältnissen	66
Kampf im Nebel und bei Dunkelheit	66
Angriff über Flüsse	68
Kampf im Wald und im Gebirge	68
V. Angriff gegen eine durch ständige Anlangen verstärkte Stellung	69
VI. Kampf „Panzer gegen Panzer"	72
VII. Verhalten beim Auftreffen auf Minen	73
VIII. Zusammenwirken mit der Stabskompanie	75
IX. Instandsetzung und Versorgung	75

Anlagen.

Anlage 1:	Erläuterungen der im Text angewandten Zeichen	77
Anlage 2:	Stärkenachweisung der mittleren Panzerkompanie an Kraftfahrzeugen (Anhalt)	78
Anlage 3:	Taktische Zahlenangaben für die mittlere Panzerkompanie	80
Anlage 4:	Führungszeichen	83
Anlage 5:	Ausführung der Flaggen	85
Anlage 6:	Erläuterung der Stoßlinie	87
Anlage 7:	Winkertafeln der Infanterie	89
Anlage 8:	Merkblatt über Bekämpfungsmöglichkeit von Panzersperren und Überwinden von Panzerhindernissen	91

	Page
c) Attack	60
Attack from March Column	63
Attack from Assembly Areas	64
d) Combat under Special Circumstances	66
Combat in Fog and Darkness	66
Attack across Rivers	68
Combat in Forests and Mountains	68
V. Attack against a Position Reinforced by Permanent Installations	69
VI. Combat "Tank vs. Tank"	72
VII. Actions upon Encountering a Minefield	73
VIII. Coordinating with the Headquarters Company	75
IX. Maintenance and Supply	75

Appendices.

Appendix 1:	Explanations of the Symbols used in the Text	77
Appendix 2:	Table of Organization of Motor Vehicles for the Medium Tank Company (Orientation)	78
Appendix 3:	Tactical Figures for the Medium Tank Company	80
Appendix 4:	Driving Signals	83
Appendix 5:	Signal Flag Designs	85
Appendix 6:	Explanation of the Axis Reference Line	87
Appendix 7:	Winter Signaling Disks of the Infantry	89
Appendix 8:	Leaflet on the Control of Tank Barriers and the Overcoming of Tank Obstacles	91

A. Wesen und Gliederung der mittleren Panzerkompanie.

1. Die *mittlere Panzerkompanie* bildet mit ihren 14 Kampfwagenkanonen (7,5 cm[11]) das Rückgrat der Panzerabteilung[12]. Diese starke Feuerkraft gilt es – im allgemeinen durch *geschlossenen Einsatz*[13] – schnell an entscheidender Stelle zu vernichtender Wirkung zu bringen.

Unübersichtlichkeit des Geländes oder die Notwendigkeit zur Verstärkung der Feuerkraft für besondere Kampfaufgaben können die Unterstellung einzelner Züge unter die leichten Kompanien erforderlich machen.

2. Die mittlere Panzerkompanie ist infolge des Kalibers und der Durchschlagskraft der Geschütze **besonders befähigt**:

> zur Vernichtung stärkerer feindlicher Widerstandsnester, von Panzerabwehrwaffen und Artillerie;

> zum Brechen feindlichen Widerstandes hinter Deckungen;

> zum Schartenbeschuß im Angriff gegen eine durch ständige Anlagen verstärkte Stellung;

> zur Vernichtung feindlicher Panzerkampfwagen.

---

[11] Hierbei handelt es sich um die 7,5 cm Kampfwagenkanone 37 L/24 auch „Kurzrohr" bzw. „Stummel" 7,5 cm. L/24 ist die Kaliberlänge, dementsprechend 24 mal 7,5 cm ergibt die Länge des Laufes.

[12] Beim deutschen Heer wurden Einheiten bestimmter Truppengattungen (wie Panzer, Artillerie, Nachrichtentruppe, etc.) in der Stärke eines Bataillons als „Abteilungen" nicht „Bataillone" bezeichnet.

[13] Siehe Glossar: Einsatz, geschlossen.

A. Nature and Composition of the Medium Tank Company.

1. The *medium tank company* with its 14 vehicle-mounted guns (7.5 cm[14]) forms the backbone of the tank battalion[15]. This strong firepower must be brought - in general by *employment of the whole unit*[16] - quickly to a decisive point and applied for destructive effect.

The complexity of the terrain or the need to increase firepower for special combat tasks may make it necessary to subordinate individual platoons to the light companies.

2. The medium tank company is **particularly suited,** due to the caliber and penetrating power of the guns:

>for the destruction of strong enemy positions, anti-tank weapons and artillery;

>to break enemy resistance behind covers;

>for embrasure bombardment in attack against a position reinforced by permanent installations;

>to destroy enemy tanks.

---

[14] This is the 7.5 cm Kampfwagenkanone 37 L/24 also "short barrel" or "stump" 7.5 cm. L/24 is the caliber length, accordingly 24 times 7.5 cm gives the length of the barrel. "Kampfwagenkanone" literally means "combat vehicle cannon".

[15] In the German army, units of some arms (like tanks, artillery, signal, etc.) with the strength of a battalion, were called "Abteilung" (literally detachments or department) not "Battalions".

[16] We could not find a satisfactory English equivalent for "geschlossenen Einsatz". See Glossary: Employment of the Whole Unit (Einsatz, geschlossen).

3. Die Kompanie gliedert sich in [1]):

    Kampfstaffel mit

        Kompanietrupp zu 2 Pz. IV,

        1 leicht. Zug zu 5 Pz. II

        Und 1. bis 3. Zug zu je 4 Pz. IV.

    Räderstaffel mit

        Kompanietrupp,

        Instandsetzungsgruppe,

        Gefechtstroß[17],

        Gepäcktroß[18],

        Sanitätstrupp.

---

[1]) Vgl. Anlage 2.

---

[17] Siehe Glossar: Gefechtstroß.

[18] Siehe Glossar: Gepäcktroß.

3. The company is composed of [1]):

    combat element[19] with

        company headquarters section of 2 Pz. IV,

        1 light platoon of 5 Pz. II

        and 1st to 3rd platoons of 4 Pz. IV each.

    wheeled vehicle element[20] with

        company headquarters section,

        maintenance section,

        combat train[21],

        baggage train[22],

        medical team.

---

[1]) See Appendix 2.

---

[19] Alternative translation could be combat echelon.
[20] Alternative translation could be wheeled vehicle echelon.
[21] See Glossary: Combat trains (Gefechtstroß).
[22] See Glossary: Baggage trains (Gepäcktroß).

B. Ausbildung.

I. Leitsätze für Erziehung und Ausbildung.
Ausbildungsziele.

4. Ziel und Umfang der Ausbildung innerhalb der mittleren Panzerkompanie bestimmt H. Dv. 470/1[23].

5. Besonderer Wert ist auf Härte, Mut, Draufgängertum und auf die Erziehung zur Kampfgemeinschaft zu legen. Diese Eigenschaften sind der Gradmesser für den Gefechtswert der Kompanie.

6. Das hochwertige, technisch schwierig zu bedienende Gerät erfordert eine eingehende und gründliche Ausbildung jedes einzelnen Mannes für seine ihm obliegenden besonderen Aufgaben.

7. Es ist daher Pflicht des **Kompanieführers** und aller unteren Vorgesetzten, sich frühzeitig ein Bild darüber zu machen, für welche Verwendung der einzelne Mann besonders geeignet ist, damit spätere Umbesetzungen vermieden werden.

Für die Auswahl werden berufliche und vormilitärische Ausbildung sowie Ergebnisse der Eignungsuntersuchung die ersten Unterlagen geben. Die Ergebnisse dieser Auswahl sind durch Fahrübungen auf Panzerfahrgestellen und Radfahrzeugen sowie durch Schieß- und Funkübungen nachzuprüfen und zu berichtigen.

---

[23] Siehe Ergänzung 1 im Anhang für den vollständigen Titel.

B. Education and Training.

I. Guidelines for Education and Training.
Educational goals.

4. The objective and scope of the medium tank company's training is set out in H. Dv. 470/1[24].

5. Particular emphasis is placed on tenacity, courage, audacity and on the education of a combat esprit de corps[25]. These characteristics are the yardstick for the combat value of the company.

6. The high-quality, technically complex to operate equipment requires in-depth and thorough training of each individual man for his special tasks.

7. It is therefore the duty of the **company commander** and the lower command to form an opinion at an early stage as to which task the individual man is particularly suitable for, in order to avoid subsequent manning changes.

For the selection, professional and pre-military training as well as the results of the aptitude test will provide the first indicators[26]. The results of this selection shall be verified and corrected by means of driving exercises on tank chassis and wheeled vehicles as well as by firing and radio exercises.

---

[24] See Supplement 1 in the Appendix for the full title.

[25] The literal translation of the German word "Kameradschaft" is "camaraderie".

[26] The literal translation of the German word "Unterlagen" is "documents".

8. Im einzelnen sind zu verlangen

a) **vom Richtschützen:** gute Augen, Veranlagung zum Entfernungsschätzen, gesunde Nerven, schnelle Auffassungsgabe.

b) vom **Panzerfahrer** und **Kraftfahrer**: technische Veranlagung, Selbstbeherrschung, Kaltblütigkeit, körperliche Härte und Anpassungsvermögen.

c) vom **Panzerfunker**: gutes Gehör, klare dialektfreie Aussprache (auf Wachsschallplatten oder durch Lautsprecher zu überprüfen), Verständnis für elektr. Vorgänge.

d) vom **Melder**: sicheres Orientierungsvermögen (auch bei Nacht), Ausdauer, Schneid und Härte.

9. Vor Beginn der Einzelausbildung am Panzerkampfwagen und in den Sondergebieten ist eine allgemeine Ausbildung des einzelnen Mannes nach H. Dv. 130/2a[27] [Ausbildungsvorschrift für die Infanterie] durchzuführen.

Diese erstreckt sich auf die Erziehung zum Soldaten, Kenntnis und Handhabung der Waffen außerhalb des Panzerkampfwagens, Kenntnis des Einsatzes und des Zusammenwirkens der anderen Waffen sowie auf die Panzer-, Gas- und Fliegerabwehr.

10. Diese militärische Grundausbildung ist während der ganzen Dienstzeit neben der Ausbildung

---

[27] Siehe Ergänzung 1 im Anhang für den vollständigen Titel.

8. The following should be sought

a) **from the gunner:** good eyes, aptitude for range estimation, healthy nerves, quick comprehension.

b) of the **tank driver** and the **motor vehicle driver**: technical ability, self-control, cold-bloodedness[28], physical resilience and adaptability.

c) from the **tank radio operator**: good hearing, clear pronunciation without dialect (to be checked on wax records or through loudspeakers), understanding of electrical processes.

d) from the **messenger**[29]: reliable orientation (also at night), endurance, guts and tenacity.

9. Before the beginning of the training with the tank and with the specializations[30], the individual aspirant is to accomplish basic training according to H. Dv. 130/2a[31] [Training Guideline for the Infantry].

This extends to his training as a soldier, his knowledge and handling of weapons outside the tank, knowledge of their use and interaction of other weapons, as well as anti-tank, anti-gas and anti-aircraft defense.

10. This basic military training shall be provided throughout the period of service, in addition to training

---

[28] From the German, "Kaltblütigkeit", implying a character trait allowing an operator to stay cool under fire and have no scruples. As you will see in this H. Dv. the driver is instructed to run over obstacles, enemy equipment and men. As such, such a character trait was required for drivers.

[29] Taken from the 1944 translation of TM 30-506: German Military Dictionary, War Department: Washington, USA, May, 1944. Modern equivalent would be "courier".

[30] Translated from the German word "Spezialgebiete" literally meaning "special areas".

[31] See Supplement 1 in the Appendix for the full title.

am Panzerkampfwagen und in den Sondergebieten weiter zu betreiben und zu vervollkommnen.

11. Bei der **Geländeausbildung** muß der Panzerschütze[32] vor allem lernen, das Gelände schnell und richtig hinsichtlich seiner Eignung für Bewegung und Schießhalt des Panzerkampfwagens zu beurteilen und auszunutzen.

Ferner muß er schnell erfassen lernen, welches Gelände günstige Deckung gegen den „Panzerfeind" bietet (Pak, Artillerie).

12. Für den **Gasspürdienst** sind 2 Gasspürtrupps in Stärke von 1 Uffz. Und 3 Mann (für Kampfstaffel und Trosse) auszubilden.

Die für diese Ausbildung angesetzten Unteroffiziere und Mannschaften müssen über guten Geruchssinn verfügen.

13. Im **Luftspähdienst** sind alle Panzerführer und einige Mannschaften der Trosse auszubilden.

II. Ausbildung am Panzerkampfwagen.

14. Die Ausbildung am Panzerkampfwagen erfolgt nach den Vorschriften:

    Panzerkampfwagen IV

        H. Dv. 470/5d[33],

        D 653/1 und 9;

---

[32] Der Panzerschütze ist nicht mit dem Richtschützen zu verwechseln! Der Panzerschütze war keine Rolle, sondern ein Rang. Es war der niedrigste Rang in der Panzertruppe.

[33] Siehe Ergänzung 1 im Anhang für die vollständigen Titel.

on the tank and special instructions.

11. During **field training,** the Panzerschütze[34] must above all learn to judge and exploit the terrain quickly and correctly estimate its suitability regarding movement and firing positions of the tank.

Furthermore, he must learn quickly which terrain offers favorable cover against the "enemy of the tank" (anti-tank guns, artillery).

12. For the **gas detection role**, 2 gas alarm sentries[35] of 1 NCO and 3 men (for combat element and trains) are to be trained.

The non-commissioned officers and teams involved in this training must have a good sense of smell.

13. All tank commanders and some troop crews shall be trained in the **air warning role**[36].

II. Training on the Tank.

14. Training on tanks is carried out according to the following regulations:

  Panzerkampfwagen IV

    H. Dv. 470/5d[37],

    D 653/1 and 9;

---

[34] "Panzerschütze" literally translated is "tank rifleman" and is not to be confused with the gunner! Panzerschütze was not a role, but a rank. German ranks were often adapted to the roles, e.g., a regular infantry man was a "Schütze". As such, "Panzerschütze" was the lowest rank within the German armored forces.

[35] The literal translation of the German word "Gasspähdienst" is "Gas scouting service".

[36] The literal translation of the German word "Luftspähdienst" is "Air scouting service".

[37] See Supplement 1 in the Appendix for the full titles.

Panzerkampfwagen II

    H. Dv. 470/5b,

    D 237,

    D 637,

    D 651/1 und 2;

Panzerschießdienst

    D 613/2, 7, 9, 10 und 14;

Panzerfunkdienst

    H. Dv. 421/4 und D 613/12;

Panzerfahrdienst

    H. Dv. 472 und D 603.

15. Bevor die **Ausbildung am Panzerkampfwagen IV** beginnt, ist eine Ausbildung am Panzerkampfwagen II im Fahren und im Schießen mit M. G. erforderlich. Erst nach Beherrschen der Grundbegriffe ist mit der Ausbildung am Panzerkampfwagen IV zu beginnen, in der Regel nach 12wöchiger Ausbildung.

16. Als **Führer, Fahrer** und **Richtschützen** im Panzerkampfwagen IV sind nur Offiziere, Unteroffiziere bzw. Gefreite auszubilden. Als Ladeschützen bzw. Funker können nach Abschluß der Rekrutenausbildung und nach der Ausbildung am Panzerkampfwagen II auch Mannschaften des 1. Dienstjahres eingeteilt werden.

Panzerkampfwagen II

    H. Dv. 470/5b,

    D 237,

    D 637,

    D 651/1 and 2;

tank gunnery

    D 613/2, 7, 9, 10 and 14;

tank radio service

    H. Dv. 421/4 and D 613/12;

tank driving

    H. Dv. 472 and D 603.

15. Before **training on the Panzerkampfwagen IV**, an instruction on the Panzerkampfwagen II in driving and firing with M. G.s is necessary. Only after mastering the basic concepts is training to begin on the Panzerkampfwagen IV, usually after 12 weeks of instruction.

16. Only officers, non-commissioned officers and corporals are to be trained as **commanders**[38], **drivers** and **gunners** in Panzerkampfwagen IV. After completion of basic training and after the training on the Panzerkampfwagen II, service members of the 1st year of service can also be assigned as loaders or radio operators.

---

[38] "Führer" is literally "leader", yet in English this is sometimes translated into "commander", e.g., "Panzerführer" is a "tank commander", "Kompanieführer" is a "company commander", although "Zugführer" is a "platoon leader".

III. Sonderausbildung.

17. Als **Panzerwarte** sind von der Kompanie in jedem Rekrutenjahrgang wenigstens 6 Mannschaften auszubilden [1]). Hierzu sind Soldaten mit abgeschlossener Berufsausbildung als Kraftfahrzeugschlosser, Mechaniker oder Elektriker einzuteilen. Die Fachausbildung hat erst zu beginnen, wenn der Soldat den Führerschein für den entsprechenden Panzerkampfwagen erworben und sich genügende Fahrfertigkeit angeeignet hat.

Die Panzerwarte erhalten ihre Fachausbildung in der Werkstatt unter Aufsicht des leitenden Offiziers (Ing.) und des Werkmeisters.

Nach Abschluß der Ausbildung müssen sie in der Lage sein, Störungen am Panzerkampfwagen rasch zu erkennen und selbstständig zu beheben, soweit die ihnen zur Verfügung stehenden Mittel dazu ausreichen.

Sie sind dann zu allen Instandsetzungsarbeiten heranzuziehen.

Während des Marsches und im Gefecht halten sich die Panzerwarte bei der Instandsetzungsgruppe auf. Die Panzerwarte sind außerdem als Hilfskrankenträger auszubilden.

---

[1]) Vgl. „Vorläufige Anweisung für den Einsatz der Instandsetzungsgruppen der Panzereinheiten und für die Ausbildung von Panzerwarten und Panzerfunkwarten".

III. Special Training.

17. At least 6 teams must be trained by the company as **tank maintenance crews** in each recruit year [1]). For this purpose, soldiers with completed professional training as motor vehicle mechanics, mechanics or electricians are to be assigned. Specialist training shall not commence until the soldier has obtained a driving license for the corresponding tank and has acquired sufficient driving skills.

The tank maintenance crews receive their specialist training in the workshop under the supervision of the chief officer (engineer) and the foreman.

After completion of the training, they must be able to detect malfunctions of the tank quickly and remedy them independently, as far as the means available to them permits this.

They must then be consulted for all maintenance work.

During march and engagements, the tank maintenance crews stay with the maintenance section. The tank maintenance crews are also to be trained as auxiliary stretcher-bearers.

---

[1]) See "Provisional instructions for the Operation of the Vehicle Maintenance Sections of the Tank Units and for the Training of Tank Maintenance Crews and Tank Radio Maintenance Crews".

18. Als **Panzerfunkwarte** sind von der Kompanie in jedem Rekrutenjahrgang wenigstens 2 Mannschaften auszubilden. Sie müssen eine abgeschlossene Berufsausbildung als Mechaniker oder Elektriker haben.

Nachdem sie ihre Funkausbildung abgeschlossen und sich im Funkdienst bewährt haben, sind sie zur weiteren Ausbildung der Nachrichtenwerkstatt zuzuweisen. Sie müssen auch technische Störungen in der funktechnischen und elektrischen Anlage des Fahrzeuges schnell erkennen und feldmäßig beheben können.

19. Für **Waffenmeistergehilfen** ist die Gesellenprüfung als Dreher, Feinmechaniker oder in ähnlichen Berufen Vorbedingung. Ihre Sonderausbildung in der Waffenmeisterei hat nach dem ersten halben Dienstjahr zu beginnen.

20. Die im **Kraftfahr- und Meldedienst** verwendeten Mannschaften sind neben der für ihre Sonderverwendung notwendigen Ausbildung nach Anordnung des Kompanieführers auch als Richtschützen oder Panzerfahrer auszubilden.

Melder müssen in der Lage sein, Skizzen anzufertigen, Meldungen abzufassen und sich im Gelände nach Skizze oder mündlicher Weisung zurechtzufinden. Das Überbringen von mündlichen und schriftlichen Meldungen auf längeren Strecken und unter wechselnden Geländeverhältnissen ist zu schulen.

18. At least 2 teams shall be trained by the company as **tank radio maintenance crews** in each recruit year. They must have completed vocational training as a mechanic or electrician.

Once they have completed their radio training and proven themselves in the radio service, they shall be assigned to the radio workshop for further training. They must also be able to quickly detect technical faults in the vehicle's radio and electrical systems and remedy them in the field.

19. For the **assistant armorer-artificer,** the journeyman's[39] examination as a lathe operator, precision mechanic or in similar professions is a prerequisite. Their special training in the armory must begin after the first half year of service.

20. Subject to the company commander discretion, in addition to the training required for their special use, the crews used in **motor-driving and message relay service** are also to be trained as gunners or tank drivers.

The messenger must be able to draw up sketches, write reports and find their way in the terrain according to sketches or verbal instructions. The delivery of oral and written reports on longer distances and under changing terrain conditions shall be trained.

---

[39] For technical crafts such as electrician or smith, a "journeyman" is a skilled worker who successfully completed an official apprenticeship qualification. Such qualifications are still in use today, both in Germany and elsewhere. The German equivalent would be "Geselle".

C. Der einzelne Panzerkampfwagen.

21. Der Panzerkampfwagen IV löst die Kampfaufträge in der Regel im Zugverbande[40]. Ausfall des Zugführers oder Halbzugführers, Abreißen der Verbindung zum Zug- und Halbzugführer und der schnell wechselnde Kampfverlauf fordern oft ein selbstständiges Handeln der einzelnen Panzerkampfwagen.

22. Die Hauptwaffe des Panzerkampfwagens IV ist die 7,5 cm Kw. K. Mit dieser bekämpft er vor allem Pak- und Geschützstellungen, Widerstandsnester hinter Deckungen und Scharten von ständigen Anlagen.

23. Das Schießen mit der 7,5 cm Kw. K. erfolgt in der Regel im Halten; Schießen während der Fahrt vermindert die Treffsicherheit und hat hohen Munitionsverbrauch zur Folge. Es ist daher nur selten gerechtfertigt.

24. Stets kommt es darauf an, aus günstiger Stellung *vor* dem Feinde das Feuer zu eröffnen.

25. Schießen auf weite Entfernungen bis 4 000 m mit dem Richtaufsatz kommt vor allem gegen feindliche Artillerie sowie gegen Massenziele in Frage,

---

[40] Der mittlere Zug besteht aus 4 Panzerkampfwagen IV. Siehe Ziffer 40.

C. The Single Tank.

21. The Panzerkampfwagen IV performs the combat mission usually as a whole platoon[41]. Loss of the platoon leader or half-platoon leader, loss of communication to the platoon and half-platoon leader and the rapidly changing course of battle often require the individual tanks to act independently.

22. The main weapon of the Panzerkampfwagen IV is the 7.5 cm Kw. K.[42]. This it employs mainly against anti-tank and gun positions, resistance nests behind cover and embrasures of fixed installations.

23. Firing with the 7.5 cm Kw. K. usually occurs while stationary; firing while driving reduces accuracy and results in high ammunition consumption. It is therefore rarely justified.

24. It is paramount in every situation to open fire from a favorable position *prior to* the enemy.

25. Firing at long distances of up to 4,000 m with the aiming device is particularly suitable against enemy artillery as well as against massed targets,

---

[41] The medium platoon consists of 4 Panzerkampfwagen IV. See Number 40.

[42] "Kw. K." means "Kampfwagenkanone", literally "combat vehicle cannon".

wenn der Panzerkampfwagen infolge von Sperren und Geländehindernissen nicht näher an das Ziel heranfahren kann.

Mit dem Turm- und Bug-M. G. greift der Panzerkampfwagen in den Feuerkampf auf nahe und nächste Entfernung gegen Ziele ohne Panzerschutz ein.

Massenziele (Kolonnen, Reserven, auffahrende Geschütze) können auch mit dem M. G. bis zu 800 m Entfernung erfolgreich bekämpft werden.

26. Jeder Mann der Besatzung muß den Kampfauftrag der Kompanie – des Zuges – genau kennen.

27. Der **Panzerführer** leitet den Feuerkampf seines Panzerkampfwagens (H. Dv. 470/5d[43], Ziff. 10).

Er hat die Feuerstellung bzw. den Schießhalt so auszusuchen, daß feindliche Panzerabwehrwaffen und Artillerie sowie alle anderen mit der Kanone zu bekämpfenden Ziele schon auf weite Entfernung unter Feuer genommen werden können und die Feuerstellung vom Feinde nicht sogleich erkannt wird. Hierbei wird der Panzerführer von dem Richtschützen und dem Panzerfahrer unterstützt.

28. Infolge Krümmung der Flugbahn können vorn kämpfende Teile mit der 7,5 cm Kw. K. überschossen werden. Die Sicherheitsbestimmungen [1]) müssen dabei beachtet werden.

---

[1]) D 613/2[44] und H. Dv. 225/2.

---

[43] Siehe Ergänzung 1 im Anhang für den vollständigen Titel.

[44] Siehe Ergänzung 1 im Anhang für den vollständigen Titel.

if the tank is unable to approach the target due to barriers and obstacles in the terrain.

The tank employs its coaxial and bow-M. G. to engage in firefights at close and proximate distances against targets without armor protection.

Massed targets (columns, reserves, moving guns) can also be fought successfully with the M. G. up to a distance of 800 m.

26. Every man of the crew must know exactly the combat mission of the company and the platoon in question.

27. The **tank commander** directs the fire of his tank (H. Dv. 470/5d[45], No. 10).

He has to select the firing position or the firing halt in such a way that enemy anti-tank weapons and artillery as well as all other targets to be fought with the cannon can already be taken under fire at a great distance, while the firing position cannot be immediately recognized by the enemy. Here the tank commander is supported by the gunner and the tank driver.

28. As a result of curvature of the flight path, overhead fire[46] can be provided with the 7.5 cm Kw. K. if friendly units[47] are fighting to the front. The safety regulations¹⁾ must be observed.

---

¹⁾ D 613/2[48] and H. Dv. 225/2.

---

[45] See Supplement 1 in the Appendix for the full title.

[46] From the German original "überschossen werden", the meaning of which primarily denotes overhead fire over friendly forces.

[47] The literal translation of the German "kämpfende Teile" would be "fighting parts".

[48] See Supplement 1 in the Appendix for the full title.

29. Ist das Ziel niedergekämpft oder sind andere Panzerkampfwagen so dicht an das Ziel herangekommen, daß ein Weiterschießen ohne Gefährdung der anderen Panzer nicht möglich ist, so eilt der Panzerkampfwagen zu neuem Schießhalt vorwärts. Dabei sind im allgemeinen Sprünge von mindestens 200 bis 300 m machen.

30. Ist die eigene Feuerstellung vom Gegner erkannt und wird der Panzerkampfwagen unter Feuer genommen, so ist rascher Stellungswechsel nach der Seite oder nach vorn geboten. Dabei haben sich Panzerführer und Panzerfahrer gegenseitig auf plötzliche Hindernisse, wie Granattrichter, aufmerksam zu machen. Der Panzerführer hat ferner dafür Sorge zu tragen, daß der Panzerkampfwagen seinen Platz in der Kampfgliederung des Zuges oder der Kompanie behält. Er wählt vorausschauend die nächste Feuerstellung aus.

31. Der **Panzerfahrer** hat seine Fahrweise so einzurichten, daß jederzeit gute Beobachtung und schnelles Zielerfassen für den Richtschützen möglich sind. Er muß seinen Panzerkampfwagen stets so zum Stehen bringen, daß Deckungen ausgenutzt werden. Am geeignetsten sind Feuerstellungen, bei denen nur das Rohr und der Turm über die Deckung ragen (Hinterhangstellungen).

In nächster Entfernung erkannte M. G. und Geschütze sind durch Niederwalzen zu vernichten. Muß

29. If the target has been put out of action or if other tanks have closed in so that further firing is not possible without endangering these units, the tank shall rush forward to a new firing position. In general, bounds of 200 to 300 m are to be made.

30. If the enemy identifies ones firing position and the tank is taken under fire, a rapid change of position to the side or forwards is required. The tank commander and the tank driver cooperate to draw each other's attention to sudden obstacles such as shell craters. The tank commander must also ensure that the tank retains its place in the tactical grouping of the platoon or company. He selects the next firing position with foresight.

31. The **tank driver** must adjust his driving style so that good observation and fast target acquisition are possible for the gunner at all times. He must always bring his tank to a standstill in such a way that cover is used. The most suitable firing positions are those where only the barrel and the turret protrude above the cover (hull-down positions).

M. G. and guns detected within immediate distance to the tank are to be destroyed by running them over. If

der Panzerfahrer hierzu von seiner Angriffsrichtung wesentlich abweisen, so bedarf es des Befehls des Panzerführers.

32. Während des Gefechtes, besonders beim Schießhalt, beobachten Panzerfahrer und Panzerfunker mit, um plötzlich auftauchenden Gegner rechtzeitig erkennen zu können.

33. Auftrag und Gelände können das Verbleiben in einer Feuerstellung zur Bekämpfung mehrerer Ziele bedingen. Das wichtigste Ziel ist stets zuerst zu bekämpfen.

Zielwechsel wird vom Panzerführer befohlen, sobald wichtigere Ziele erkannt werden. Der Panzerführer ist dafür verantwortlich, daß nicht Ziele beschossen werden, die bereits von anderen Panzerkampfwagen des Verbandes bekämpft werden. Keine Granate darf unnötig verschossen werden.

34. Bei geringfügigen Störungen und Schäden im Gefecht, auch bei geminderter Fahrfähigkeit, hat der Panzerkampfwagen weiterzukämpfen.

35. Wird der Panzerkampfwagen während des Gefechtes bewegungsunfähig, so ist vom haltenden Wagen aus weiterzukämpfen. Solange der Panzerkampfwagen noch schießen kann, bleibt die Besatzung im Wagen. Nur Beschuß durch panzerbrechende Waffen oder Artillerie kann zum Verlassen des

the tank driver must substantially change his direction of attack, the order of the tank commander is required.

32. During combat, especially at the firing halt, tank drivers and tank radio operators shall also assist target and terrain surveillance in order to facilitate the timely detection of suddenly appearing enemies.

33. Mission and terrain may require the tank to remain a firing position to engage multiple targets. The most important target is always to be engaged first.

Changing targets is ordered by the tank commander as soon as more important targets are detected. The tank commander is responsible for ensuring that targets are not fired at that are already being fought by other tanks of the unit. No shell may be fired unnecessarily.

34. In the event of minor disruptions and damage during engagements, even with reduced driving ability, the tank shall continue to fight on.

35. If the tank becomes immobile during engagements, fighting shall continue from the halted vehicle. As long as the tank can still fire, the crew remains in the vehicle. Only fire from armor-piercing weapons or artillery may force the crew to leave the

Wagens durch den Notausstieg zwingen. Handwaffen sind hierbei mitzunehmen.

Hilfe durch andere Panzerkampfwagen zum Abschleppen in eine Deckung darf nur für kurze Strecken und auf Befehl des Zugführers gewährt werden.

Zwingt die Lage zum Zerstören des Panzerkampfwagens, so ist diese nach H. Dv. 470/5b[49] durchzuführen; M. G., Handwaffen, Funkgerät und andere wichtige Teile sind zu bergen.

---

[49] Siehe Ergänzung 1 im Anhang für den vollständigen Titel.

vehicle through the emergency exit. Small arms[50] are to be taken with the crew on bail outs.

Help from other tanks to tow the immobilized tank into cover may only be provided for short distances and only by order of the platoon leader.

If the situation forces the destruction of the Panzerkampfwagen, then this is to be accomplished according to H. Dv. 470/5b[51]; M. G., small arms, radio and other important parts are to be recovered.

---

[50] The literal translation of "Handwaffen" would be "hand weapons", which means "small arms".

[51] See Supplement 1 in the Appendix for the full title.

D. Der Zug.

Allgemeines.

36. Der Zugführer ist für die Gefechtsbereitschaft seines Zuges verantwortlich.

Er ist der Gehilfe des Kompanieführers bei der Ausbildung und führt den Zug nach seinen Befehlen durch Funk, Beispiel, Zeichen oder Flaggen.

37. Bei der Befehlsgebung durch Funk befiehlt der Zugführer an den gesamten Zug oder an die Halbzüge (Gruppen)[52]. Die Bestätigung erhält er entweder durch die sofortige Ausführung oder durch Zeichen [1]).

38. **Zeichen** werden durch Hand oder Flaggen [2]), nachts durch farbiges Licht gegeben, im Gefecht nur durch Flaggen. Befehle durch Zeichen werden sofort bei Erkennen ausgeführt sowie durch Wiederholen weitergegeben und dadurch bestätigt.

Bei Zeichengebung aus dem Halten gilt das Erscheinen der Flagge als Ankündigungs-, das Verschwinden als Ausführungskommando. Das Führerfahrzeug zieht die Flagge erst dann ein, wenn es von dem anderen Fahrzeug seiner Einheit Bestätigung hat.

---

[1]) Im übrigen siehe D 613/12[53].
[2]) Siehe Anlagen 4 und 5.

---

[52] Halbzüge für die mittlere Panzerkompanie, Gruppen für die leichte Panzerkompanie. Siehe Glossar.

[53] Siehe Ergänzung 1 im Anhang für den vollständigen Titel.

D. The Platoon.

General Information.

36. The platoon leader is responsible for the combat readiness of his platoon.

He is the assistant of the company commander during training and guides the platoon according to his orders by radio, example, signals or flags.

37. When issuing orders by wireless radio communication, the platoon leader commands the whole platoon or the half-platoons (sections)[54]. The confirmation is received either by immediate execution [of his orders] or by signal [1]).

38. Signals are given by hand or flags [2]), at night by colored light, and during engagements only by flags. Commands by signals are executed immediately upon recognition, as well as being passed on and thereby confirmed.

In the case of signals during a stop, the appearance of the flag is considered an announcement command, the disappearance as an execution command. The commander's vehicle retracts the flag only after it has received confirmation from the other vehicle in its unit.

---

[1]) For the rest see D 613/12[55].
[2]) See Appendices 4 and 5.

---

[54] Half-platoons for the medium tank company, sections for the light tank company. See Glossary.

[55] See Supplement 1 in the Appendix for the full title.

39. Der **Halbzugführer** (bei leichtem Zuge der Gruppenführer) ist für seine beiden Panzerkampfwagen verantwortlich. Er führt den Halbzug bzw. die Gruppe im Gefecht durch Beispiel und leitet das Feuer durch Richtungsschüsse.

a) Der mittlere Panzerkampfwagenzug.

40. Der **Zug** besteht aus 4 Panzerkampfwagen IV und gliedert sich in zwei Halbzüge. Den ersten Halbzug führt der Zugführer, den zweiten Halbzug der Halbzugführer.

1. Formen und Bewegungen.

41. Antreten ohne Fahrzeuge.

Ohne Fahrzeuge tritt der Zug auf das Kommando: „**In Linie – angetreten!**" nach Bild 1, auf das Kommando: „**In Linie zu zwei Gliedern – angetreten!**" nach Bild 2 besatzungsweise an.

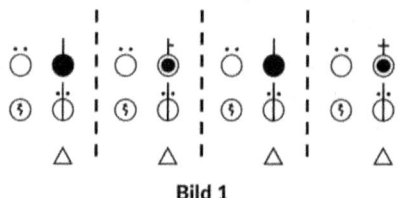

Bild 1
Zugbesatzung in „Linie zu 3 Gliedern" angetreten [1]).

---

[1]) Zeichenerklärungen siehe Anlage 1.

39. The **half-platoon leader** (in the case of a light platoon, the section leader[56]) is responsible for his two tanks. He leads the half-platoon or the section in combat by example and designates targets with his own fire[57].

a) The Medium Tank Platoon.

40. The **platoon** consists of 4 Panzerkampfwagen IV and is divided into two half-platoons. The first half-platoon is led by the platoon leader, the second half-platoon by the half-platoon leader.

1. Formations and Movements.

41. Falling in without vehicles.

Without vehicles, the platoon will present itself on the command: **"In line – fall in [at attention]**[58]**"** according to Fig. 1, and on the command: **"In line two ranks – fall in [at attention]"** according to Figure 2.

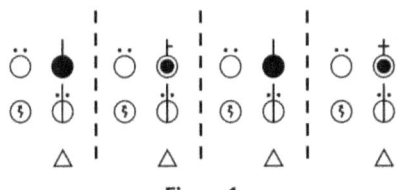

Figure 1
Platoon crew in "line of 3 ranks" at attention [1]).

---

[1]) Explanations of symbols see Appendix 1.

---

[56] The German word "Gruppenführer" (literally "group leader") was used in both infantry and tank units. The English translation for infantry units would be the "squad leader". In the case of tank units, the correct term is "section leader". See FM 17-10 Armored Force Field Manual from 1942, p. 205.

[57] The literal translation of the German word "Richtungsschüsse" would be "directing shots".

[58] The TM 30-506 German Military Dictionary by the US War Department from 1944 translates "angetreten" with "fall in at attention". Interestingly FM 17-71 from the US War Department used for crew drill on half-tracks from 1943 just uses "fall in". Reibert: Dienstunterricht im Heere from 1940 for the rifleman in the rifle company notes that after the command "angetreten", the men place themselves into their correct position shortly before they are at attention on the command of "stillgestanden".

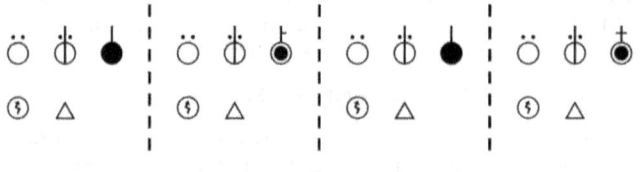

Bild 2
Zugbesatzung in „Linie zu 2 Gliedern" angetreten [1]).

42. Auf das Kommando: **„An die – Fahrzeuge!"** begibt sich jede Besatzung auf den kürzesten Wege an ihr Fahrzeug und tritt nach H. Dv. 470/5d[59] an.

43. Formen des Zuges sind:

Versammlungsform

    Linie (Bild 3),

    Reihe (Bild 4);

Marschform

    Reihe,

    Doppelreihe (Bild 5);

Gefechtsform

    Geöffnete Reihe,

    Doppelreihe,

    Keil (Bild 6),

    Geöffnete Linie.

---

[1]) Zeichenerklärungen siehe Anlage 1.

---

[59] Siehe Ergänzung 1 im Anhang für den vollständigen Titel.

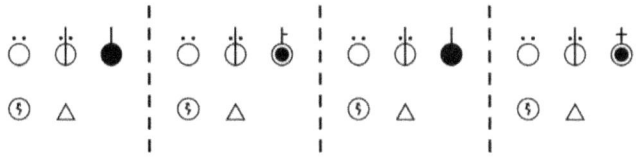

Figure 2
Platoon crew in "line of 2 ranks" at attention [1]).

42. On the command: **"To the vehicles"**, each crew shall take the shortest route to their vehicle and proceed in accordance to H. Dv. 470/5d[60].

43. Formations of the platoon are:

Assembly formation

    line (Figure 3),

    column (Figure 4);

marching formations

    column,

    double column (Figure 5);

combat formations

    open column,

    double column,

    wedge (Figure 6),

    open line.

---

[1]) Explanations of symbols see Appendix 1.

---

[60] See Supplement 1 in the Appendix for the full title.

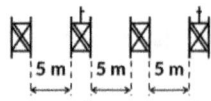

Bild 3
Der Zug in „Linie" (Versammlungsform). – Im Gefecht
Zwischenraum von Fahrzeug zu Fahrzeug etwa 50 m.

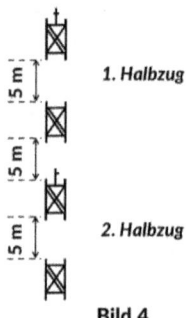

Bild 4
Der Zug in „Reihe" (Versammlungsform). – Bei Marsch und
Gefecht Abstand von Fahrzeug zu Fahrzeug etwa 25 m.

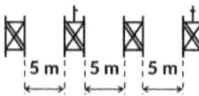

Figure 3
The platoon in "line" (assembly formation). - In combat, the distance between vehicles is about 50m.

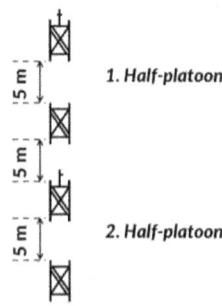

1. Half-platoon
2. Half-platoon

Figure 4
The platoon in "column" (assembly formation). - For march and combat, the distance from vehicle to vehicle is about 25m.

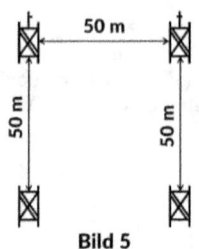

Bild 5
Der Zug in „Doppelreihe".

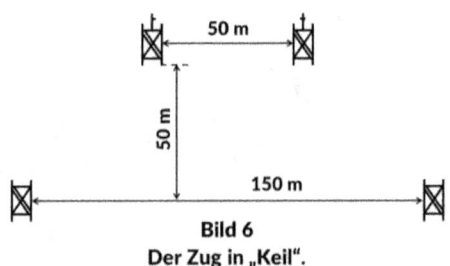

Bild 6
Der Zug in „Keil".

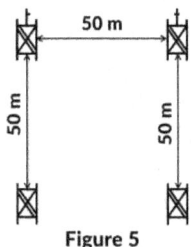

Figure 5
The platoon in "double column".

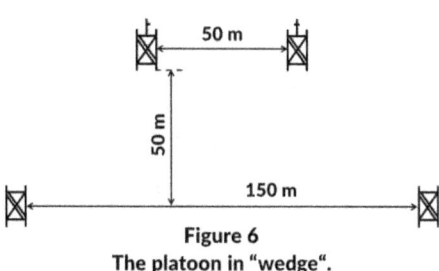

Figure 6
The platoon in "wedge".

44. Die angegebenen Zwischenräume und Abstände müssen bei formalen Bewegungen eingehalten werden. Im Gefecht dienen sie als Anhalt. Lage, Gelände, Auftrag, Feindeinwirkung können zu Abweichungen zwingen.

Soll bei formalen Bewegungen von den festgesetzten Abständen abgewichen werden, so ist dies besonders zu befehlen, z. B. „**Halbe (doppelte) Abstände!**" oder Zeichen**: „Abstände verringern (erweitern)!"**

Formveränderungen werden nach Bild 7 bis 12 ausgeführt. Aufmärsche aus der Bewegung zur Linie sind nicht zu üben.

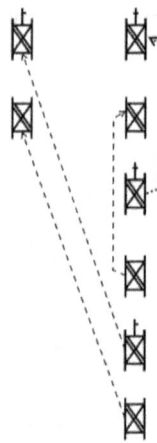

Bild 7
Formveränderung aus „Reihe" zur „Doppelreihe".
[Die gepunktete Linie war im Original nicht vorhanden. Danke an Nicholas Moran.]

44. The specified spaces and distances must be observed during formal movements. In an engagement, they serve as a guideline. Location, terrain, mission, enemy influence can force changes in spacing.

If the set distances during formal movements are to be changed, special instructions, e.g. **"Half (double) distances"** or **"Increase (decrease) distances"** will be given.

Formation changes are carried out as shown in Figures 7 to 12. Assembly from line formations are not to be practiced.

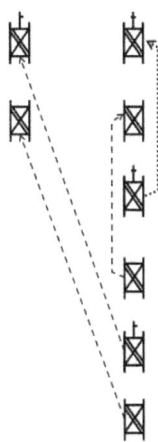

Figure 7
Change of formation from "column" to "double column". [The dotted line was not present in the original. Thanks to Nicholas Moran.]

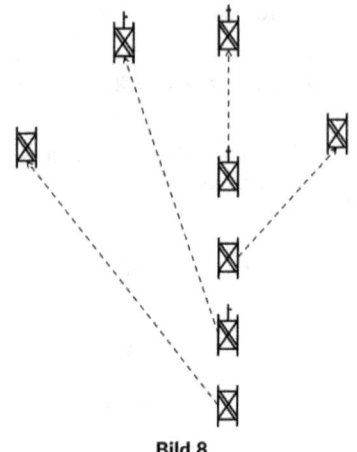

Bild 8
Formveränderung aus „Reihe" zum „Keil".

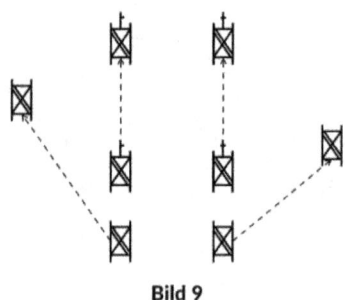

Bild 9
Formveränderung aus „Doppelreihe" zum „Keil".

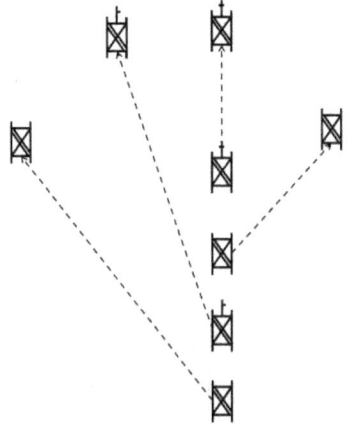

Figure 8
Change of formation from "column" to "wedge".

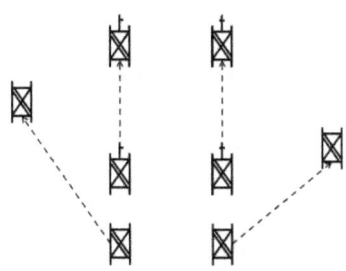

Figure 9
Change of formation from "double column" to "wedge".

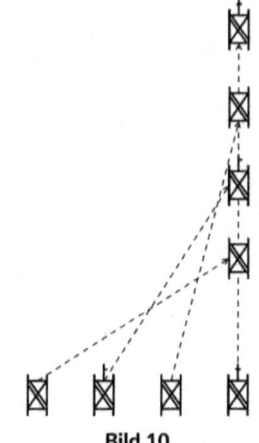

Bild 10
Formveränderung aus „Linie" zur „Reihe".

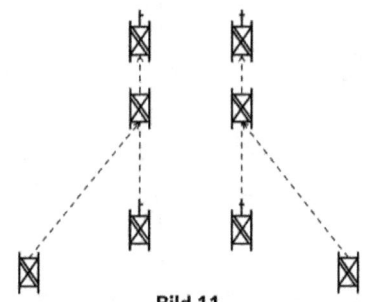

Bild 11
Formveränderung aus „Keil" zum „Doppelreihe".

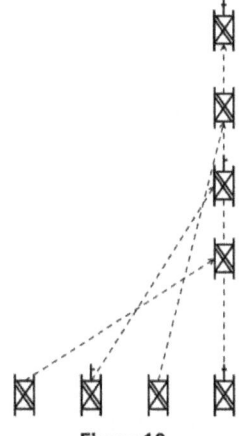

Figure 10
Change of formation from "line" to "column".

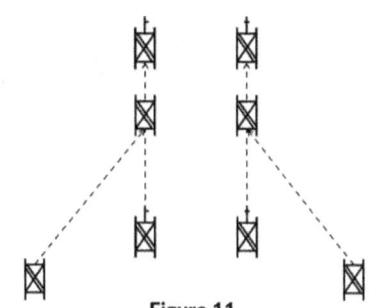

Figure 11
Change of formation from "wedge" to "double column".

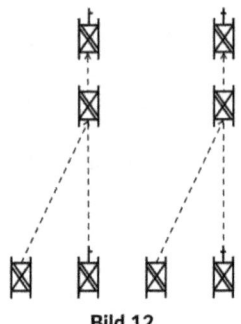

Bild 12
Formveränderung aus „Linie" zum „Doppelreihe".

45. Im Gefecht wählt der Zugführer entsprechend der Lage und dem Gelände die Form für den Zug selbstständig.

46. Zugführer find nur bei formalen Bewegungen an ihren vorgeschriebenen Platz gebunden. Im Gefecht wählen sie ihre Plätze je nach Lage und Gelände dort, wo sie den Kampf am besten führen können.

47. Bewegungen werden auf Funkkommando, Befehl oder Zeichen des Zugführers ausgeführt.

48. Alle Panzerkampfwagen fahren auf Befehl oder Zeichen gleichmäßig an und zunächst geradeaus. Soll gleichzeitig mit dem Anfahren eine Formveränderung vorgenommen werden, so ist erst die Form und dann das Anfahren zu befehlen. Abstände, Zwischenräume und Form werden im Fahren genommen.

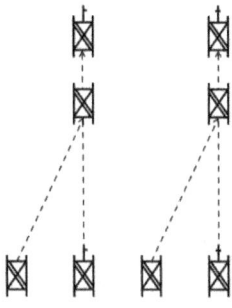

Figure 12
Change of formation from "line" to "double column".

45. During an engagement, the platoon leader will choose the formation of the platoon according to the situation and terrain.

46. Platoon leaders are only bound to their prescribed positions during formal movements. During an engagement they are free to choose their positions according to the situation and terrain from where they can best conduct the engagement.

47. Movements are carried out on radio command, command or signal by the platoon leader.

48. All tanks start at the same speed on command or signal and go straight ahead at first. If a formation change is to be carried out at the same time as the start-up, the formation order is given first, followed by the start-up command. While driving, the vehicles then take their positions, keeping in mind spacing and their relative position within the formation.

49. Die Fahrgeschwindigkeit bei formalen Bewegungen beträgt 20 km/std. Abweichungen sind zu befehlen. Bei Aufmärschen erhöhen die aufmarschierenden Teile ihre Geschwindigkeit; die Teile, auf welche dabei aufmarschiert wird, verringern ihre Geschwindigkeit bis zur Vollendung des Aufmarsches.

50. Beim Abbrechen behalten die Teile, auf welche abgebrochen wird, die bisherige Geschwindigkeit bei. Die abbrechenden Teile verringern ihre Geschwindigkeit entsprechend und fahren auf kürzesten Wege auf ihren Platz.

51. Bei **Marschrichtungsänderungen** befiehlt der Zugführer: „**Wir folgen!**" oder „**Marschrichtung ....!**" mit Angabe des Richtungspunktes oder der Kompaßzahl.

Soll gleichzeitig eine Formveränderung durchgeführt werden, so ist erst die Marschrichtung, **dann** die neue Form zu befehlen.

52. Auf das Zeichen: „**Kehrt! – Marsch!**" führt jedes Fahrzeug die Kehrtwendung für sich so schnell und kurz aus, wie es Gelände und Laufwerk gestatten. Bei formalen Bewegungen ist die Kehrtwendung linksherum auszuführen.

Bei Kehrtwendungen im **Gefecht** bleiben Zugführer und Halbzugführer zunächst auf ihren feindwärtigen[61] Plätzen. Die Türme bleiben auf den Feind gerichtet. Sobald sich der Zug genügend vom

---

[61] Feindwärts: in Richtung auf den Feind.

49. The driving speed for formal movements shall be 20 kph[62]. Deviations therefrom need to be ordered. During form-up[63], the joining elements increase their speed; while the already assembled elements decrease their speed. This is done until the joining elements have caught up and the assembly is complete.

50. When breaking off [from the formation], the remaining elements retain their speed. The breaking elements reduce their speed accordingly and drive on shortest way to their new position.

51. When the **march direction changes,** the platoon leader says: **"We follow!"** or **"march direction . . . . !"** with indication of the direction point or the compass heading.

If a change of formation is to be carried out at the same time, first the marching direction is ordered, **followed** by the new formation.

52. On the signal: **"Turn! - March",** each vehicle turns around as quickly and promptly as terrain and running gear allow. In the case of formal movements, turn left.

During turnarounds in an **engagement,** platoon leaders and half-platoon leaders initially remain in their positions facing the enemy. The turrets remain pointed at the enemy. As soon as the platoon has moved enough from the

---

[62] Kilometers per hour: One kph equals 0.62 mph (miles per hour).

[63] "Form-up" from the German "Aufmarsch" is usually the assembly of troops. Yet, in this case it is about following up to the previous elements.

Feinde gelöst hat, setzt sich der Zugführer wieder an die Spitze des Zuges. Die Waffen sind in die neue Fahrtrichtung zu schwenken. Der Halbzugführer nimmt selbstständig seinen Platz ein.

Wird auf Straßen oder Wegen kehrtgemacht, so ist nach der Kehrtwendung in der Regel scharf rechts heranzufahren, um die Führer vorfahren zu lassen.

53. Auf das Zeichen: „**Volle Deckung!**" fahren alle Panzerkampfwagen selbstständig in die nächste Deckung und suchen Schutz gegen Beobachtung und Wirkung aus der Luft und auf der Erde. Die Verbindung zum Zugführer wird beibehalten, so daß sofortiges Wiederantreten gewährleistet ist.

54. Bei dem Kommando: „**Halt!**" schließt der Zug nur auf, wenn dem Zeichen zum Halten das Zeichen „**Langsamer fahren!**" vorausgeht.

2. Der mittlere Zug im Gefecht.

55. Jeder Zug bildet eine **Kampfeinheit** innerhalb der Kompanie.

Einsatz und Unterstellung von Halbzügen bilden die Ausnahme, sie können erfolgen

> zur Unterstützung der leichten Kompanien in unübersichtlichen Gelände,
>
> zur Unterstützung von Stoßtrupps beim Angriff gegen eine durch ständige Anlagen verstärkte Stellung,
>
> beim Kampf unter besonderen Verhältnissen.

enemy to have disengaged, the platoon leaders moves to the head of the platoon again. The weapons are to be swung in the new driving direction. The half-platoon leader takes his place independently.

If the platoon reverses direction on roads or paths, the tanks will pull over, usually to the right side of the road, to allow the commanders tank to pass.

53. On the signal: **"Full cover!"** all tanks drive independently into the nearest cover and look for protection against observation and effect from the air and on the ground. The communication to the platoon leader is maintained so that the unit can immediately form up[64] again.

54. With the command: **"Stop!"** the platoon only catches up if the stop signal is preceded by the signal **"Slow down!"**.

2. The Medium Platoon in an Engagement.

55. Each platoon forms a **combat unit** within the company.

Employment and subordination of half-platoons are the exception, they can take place

> to support the light companies in complex[65] terrain,
>
> to support assault detachments in their attack against a position reinforced by permanent installations,
>
> in combat under special circumstances.

---

[64] The German original "Wiederantreten" can also be translated as "to fall in again".

[65] From the German "unübersichtliches Terrain", translating to a complex, confusing, convoluted and unclear terrain.

56. Während des Angriffs wird der Zug durch Funk geführt. Der Zugführer gibt im allgemeinen die Feuerbefehle für die Halbzüge (D 613/12[66]).

Er kann das Feuer aller Panzerkampfwagen durch Funk oder durch Richtungsschüsse seines Panzerkampfwagens auf bestimmte Ziele lenken und zusammenfassen.

57. Stellt sich die Kompanie zum Angriff bereit, so ist die Gefechtsbereitschaft des Zuges schnell herzustellen, der Zugführer gibt hierzu die notwendigen Anordnungen.

Stets ist die Verbindung mit dem Kompanieführer aufrechtzuerhalten.

58. Auf Grund des Kompaniebefehls gibt der Zugführer den Angriffsbefehl.

Er muß enthalten:

a) Feind (Abwehrwaffen, feindliche Panzer, Artillerie),

b) Gelände und Hindernisse,

c) Auftrag der Kompanie oder der Einheit, der der Zug unterstellt ist,

d) Zusammenwirken mit anderen Waffen, Lage eigener bereits eingesetzter Truppen,

e) Auftrag des Zuges, Angriffsziel, Platz innerhalb der Einheit, Art der Gefechtsführung,

f) Anschluß[67], Trennungslinien und Mittellinie,

g) Zeitpunkt für Antreten,

h) Verhalten nach Erreichen des Angriffszieles.

---

[66] Siehe Ergänzung 1 im Anhang für den vollständigen Titel.

[67] Siehe Glossar.

56. During the attack, the platoon will be directed via wireless communication. The platoon leader generally gives the fire orders for the half-platoons (D 613/12[68]).

He can direct the fire of all tanks by radio or by directing shots from his tank on certain targets and thus concentrate his firepower.

57. If the company is getting ready to attack, the readiness of the platoon has to be established rapidly, for which the platoon leader shall give the necessary orders.

The communication with the company commander must always be maintained.

58. Based on his company's orders, the platoon leader gives the order to attack.

> It must contain:
>
> a) Enemy (defensive weapons, enemy tanks, artillery),
>
> b) terrain and obstacles,
>
> c) the mission of the company or unit to which the platoon is subordinated to,
>
> d) coordination with other weapons, situation of the friendly troops already committed,
>
> e) mission of the platoon, objective, position within the unit, type of combat command,
>
> f) contact[69] ,unit boundaries and center line,
>
> g) time of the fall in[70],
>
> h) behavior after reaching the objective.

---

[68] See Supplement 1 in the Appendix for the full title.

[69] From German "Anschluß", which in this case is translated with "contact". It refers to a person, vehicle or unit which was used as a reference point. For further information see the Glossary.

[70] See the footnote at Number 41.

59. Meist wird es Aufgabe des Zuges sein, das Vorbrechen der leichten Panzerkampfwagen und deren Einbruch[71] in den Feind aus günstigen Stellungen zu überwachen.

Rascher Stellungswechsel der Halbzüge ist hierbei geboten. Das Vorfahren in einen neuen Feuerhalt hat mit größtmöglicher Geschwindigkeit zu erfolgen.

60. Der Zugführer wählt die Feuerstellungen so, daß er überhöhend auf weite Entfernungen wirken und Feindziele, die den leichten Kompanien bereits auf weiten Entfernungen Widerstand entgegensetzen, niederkämpfen oder blenden kann.

61. Panzerabwehrwaffen und Artillerie sind durch zusammengefaßtes Feuer des Zuges oder der Halbzüge zu bekämpfen.

62. Im weiteren Verlauf des Angriffs folgt der Zug derart, daß ein Halbzug steht und überwacht, während der andere die nächste Stellung fährt.

Ein gleichzeitiges Fahren beider Halbzüge bildet die Ausnahme.

63. Schnelle Annäherung an den Feind und Auswahl der ersten Feuerstellung sind besonders wichtig.

Im steten Wechsel zwischen Feuer und Bewegung dringt der Zug in den Gegner ein.

---

[71] Einbruch: Der Einbruch ist nicht mit dem Durchbruch zu verwechseln. Beim Einbruch war der Angriff gegen die vorderste feindliche erfolgreich. Der Einbruch ist eine notwendige Vorstufe des Durchbruchs.

59. In most cases it will be the task of the platoon to overwatch the assault[72] of the light tanks and their break-in[73] of the enemy line from favorable positions.

A rapid change of position of the half-platoons is required. The relocation into a new firing halt has to take place with the greatest possible speed.

60. The platoon leader chooses the firing positions in such a way that he can act from a long distance with a commanding view and is able to put out of action or blind enemy targets that engaged the light companies at long distances.

61. Anti-tank weapons and artillery shall be engaged by the combined fire of the platoon or half-platoons.

62. Further on during the attack the platoon follows in such a way that one half-platoon stands and monitors, while the other moves to the next position.

Simultaneous movement of both half-platoons is the exception.

63. A rapid advance on the enemy and selection of the first firing position are particularly important.

The platoon penetrates the enemy lines by a constant shift between fire and movement.

---

[72] Note "Vorbrechen" literally means "pre-breakage", yet in this case it means moving/rushing forward.

[73] Break-in: The break-in should not be confused with the penetration. A break-in means that the attack against the first line of the enemy defense was successful. The break-in is the necessary precursor to the penetration.

64. Beim **Kampf gegen feindlichen Panzer** ist die schnelle Eröffnung wirksamen Feuers aus günstiger Feuerstellung von ausschlaggebender Bedeutung.

Hat der Panzerfeind den eigenen Verband bei der Einnahme der Feuerstellung noch nicht erkannt, muß der Zugführer einen Feuerüberfall[74] mit allen Waffen anstreben.

Bei überraschenden Zusammenstoß mit feindlichen Panzern auf nahe Entfernungen hat jeder Wagen des Zuges selbständig, auch in Bewegung, das Feuer aufzunehmen.

65. Ist ein mittlerer Zug einer leichten Kompanie unterstellt, die in deckungslosem Gelände überraschend auf feindlichen in Stellung befindliche Panzer stößt, so wird es meist zweckmäßig sein, den Feind beschleunigt durch Beschuß mit Nebel zu blenden, um der leichten Kompanie das Loslösen und den erneuten Einsatz an anderer Stelle zu ermöglichen.

66. Gerät der Zug überraschend in starkes Feuer feindlicher Panzerkampfwagen oder vor eine Panzersperre, so ist unter Verwendung von Nebel abzudrehen und die Bekämpfung des Gegners unter günstigeren Bedingungen wieder aufzunehmen. Der Gegner ist möglichst aus der Flanke anzugreifen, Sperren sind zu umgehen.

67. Lebende Ziele und nichtpanzerbrechende Waffen werden mit M. G. und Sprenggranaten und im Nahkampf auch durch Niederwalzen mit dem Fahrzeug bekämpft.

---

[74] Siehe Glossar: Feuerüberfall.

64. In combat against enemy tanks a rapid commencement of effective fire from a favorable firing position is of crucial importance.

If the enemy tank [unit][75] has not yet recognized the friendly formation as it takes its firing position, the platoon leader must strive for surprise fire[76] with all weapons.

In the event of a surprising encounter with enemy tanks at close range, each of the platoon's vehicles must engage and fire independently, even in motion.

65. If a medium platoon is subordinated to a light company which, in uncovered terrain, unexpectedly encounters enemy tanks in position, it will usually be expedient to blind the enemy with smoke in order to enable the light company to disengage and employ it elsewhere.

66. If the platoon is unexpectedly subjected to heavy fire by enemy tanks or in front of a tank barrier, it shall disengage using smoke and the engagement will be resumed under more favorable conditions. The enemy if possible is to be attacked from the flank, barriers are to be circumvented.

67. Living targets and non-armor-piercing weapons are engaged with M. G. and explosive shells and, during close combat, also by running them over with the vehicle.

---

[75] The literal translation of the German word "Panzerfeind" is "armor(ed) enemy".

[76] The literal translation of the German word "Feuerüberfall" would be "firing raid", although in this case "Überfall" refers to the surprise effect. See Glossary: Surprise Fire (Feuerüberfall).

Stößt der Zug auf feindliche Massenziele (Reserven, zurückflutende Teile oder anmarschierende Kolonnen), eröffnet er sofort das Feuer. **Alle** Waffen feuern mit höchster Geschwindigkeit. Die Kanonen schießen mit Sprenggranaten. Noch haltender Gegner wird niedergewalzt.

68. Beim Angriff gegen ständige Anlagen wird der einzeln eingesetzte Pz. Kpfw.-Zug stets auf enges Zusammenwirken mit der zu Fuß angreifenden Truppe angewiesen. In der Regel wird der Zug der angreifendenden Einheit unterstellt. Er erhält durch sie seine Aufgaben und Ziele zugewiesen.

Lassen Gelände und Angriffsplan den geschlossenen Einsatz des Zuges zu, unterstützen sich die einzelnen Panzerkampfwagen bei der Annäherung durch wechselseitiges Niederhalten. Der Zug geht so weit vor, daß er aus naher Entfernung die Waffen in den Schartenblenden wirksam niederkämpfen kann. Haben die Stoßtrupps unter dem Feuerschutz des Zuges eine Kampfanlage genommen, so übernimmt der Zug den Schutz für ihr weiteres Vorgehen durch Abriegelung nach der Flanke und Tiefe.

69. Ist das **Öffnen von Sperren** [1]) dem mittleren Zuge allein nicht möglich, so unterstützt er den Angriff der Schützen oder Pioniere durch Nebel- und

---

[1]) Vgl. Anlage 8.

If the platoon encounters enemy massed targets (reserves, disengaging elements[77] or approaching columns), it immediately opens fire. **All** weapons engage with the highest rate of fire. The [main] guns[78] fire explosive shells. Enemy units holding their positions are to be run over.

68. When attacking permanent installations, the individually committed tank platoon relies on close coordination with the troops attacking on foot. As a rule, the platoon is subordinated to the attacking unit. It is assigned its tasks and objectives by them.

If the terrain and the attack plan allow the employment of the platoon as a whole, the individual tanks support each other during the approach by alternatingly covering each other. The platoon advances until it can effectively overpower the weapons in the embrasures from a close distance. If the assault detachments have captured a defensive installation[79] under the protective fire of the platoon, the platoon takes over the protection of their further actions by locking off the flank and depth.

69. If the **opening of barriers** [1]) is not possible by the medium platoon alone, it supports the attack of the riflemen or engineers with smoke and

---

[1]) See Appendix 8.

---

[77] The literal translation of the German "zurückflutende Teile", would be "back flooding/flowing parts".

[78] From the German word "Kanone", literally translating to cannon.

[79] The literal translation of the German word "Kampfanlage" would be "combat facility".

Sprenggranaten. Gegen Eisensperren wirken die Panzerkampfwagen auch mit Panzergranaten.

70. Beim **Kampf um Ortschaften** greift der Zug feindliche Widerstandsnester in Häusern und hinter Sperren an. Er ist in der Lage, durch Nebel den Feind zu blenden und das Heranarbeiten der Schützen zu unterstützen.

71. Wird ein **Angriff bei Nebel**, in **unübersichtlichen Gelände** oder in der **Dämmerung** durchgeführt, so sind Abstände und Zwischenräume zu verkürzen. Beim Aufreißen des Nebels sind die Abstände und Zwischenräume rasch wieder zu erweitern.

Neben dem Fahren nach dem Kurskreisel[80] kann durch besonders verabredete farbige Leuchtzeichen mit Taschenlampen der Zusammenhang im Zuge sichergestellt werden.

72. Verschärfte Aufmerksamkeit der Besatzungen und Feuerschutz der einzelnen Wagen untereinander sind besonders wichtig, um der Gefahr plötzlicher Nahangriffe des Feindes zu begegnen.

Im einzelnen regelt das Verhalten der Besatzungen bei Nahangriffen und bei bewegungsunfähigen Pz. Kpfw. H. Dv. 470/5b[81], Ziffer 81 bis 83.

b) Der leichte Zug.

73. Der leichte Zug besteht aus dem Führerfahrzeug und zwei Gruppen, die von je einem Gruppenführer geführt werden.

---

[80] Ein Kurskreisel ist ein Gyroskop.

[81] Siehe Ergänzung 1 im Anhang für den vollständigen Titel.

explosive shells. Against iron barriers the tanks can also use anti-tank shells.

70. In the **battle within built up areas**[82] the platoon attacks resistance nests in houses and behind barriers. It is able to blind the enemy through smoke and support the approach of the riflemen.

71. If an **attack is** carried out **in fog**, in **confusing terrain** or at **dusk**, distances and spaces are to be shortened. When the fog lifts, the separation [between the tanks] must be quickly extended again.

In addition to navigating with the course gyro[83], unit cohesion can be ensured by specially arranged colored illuminated signals with flashlights.

72. Increased attention by crews and covering fire between the vehicles are particularly important to counter the risk of sudden close-range attacks by the enemy.

In detail, crew behavior during close assaults and with immobile tanks is regulated in 470/5b[84], Number 81 to 83.

b) The Light Platoon.

73. The light platoon consists of the commander's vehicle and two sections, each led by a section leader.

---

[82] The original handbook describes this as "Ortschaften", which is a generic term for (small) populated areas but can also be directly translated as settlements or towns.

[83] A course gyro is a gyroscope.

[84] See Supplement 1 in the Appendix for the full title.

74. Ohne Fahrzeuge tritt der Zug auf das Kommando „**In Linie - angetreten!**" nach Bild 1, auf das Kommando:

„**In Linie zu zwei Gliedern - angetreten!**" auf Bild 2 besatzungsweise an.

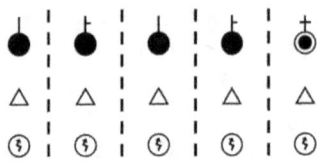

Bild 1
Zugbesatzung in „Linie zu 3 Gliedern" angetreten [1]).

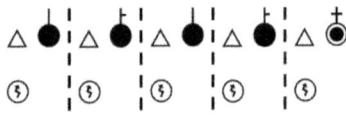

Bild 2
Zugbesatzung in „Linie zu 2 Gliedern" angetreten [1]).

75. Auf das Kommando: „**An die - Fahrzeuge!**" begibt sich jede Besatzung auf den kürzesten Wege an ihr Fahrzeug und tritt nach H. Dv. 470/5b[85] an.

---

[1]) Zeichenerklärung siehe Anlage 1.

---

[85] Siehe Ergänzung 1 im Anhang für den vollständigen Titel.

74. Without vehicles the platoon steps on the command **"In line – fall in!"** according to Figure 1; on the command:

"In line by two ranks – fall in!" in Figure 2, crew by crew.

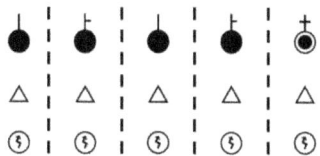

Figure 1
Platoon crew in "line of 3 ranks" at attention [1]).

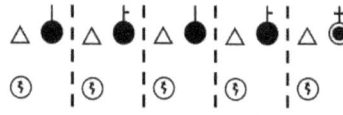

Figure 2
Platoon crew in "line of 2 ranks" at attention [1]).

75. On the command: **"To the – vehicles"**, each crew shall make their way to their vehicle by the shortest route and proceeds in accordance with H. Dv. 470/5b[86].

[1]) Explanation of symbols see Appendix 1.

---

[86] See Supplement 1 in the Appendix for the full title.

1. Formen und Bewegungen.

76. Formen des Zuges sind:

Versammlungsform
> Linie (Bild 3),
> Reihe (Bild 4);

Marschform
> Reihe,
> Doppelreihe (Bild 5);

Gefechtsform
> Geöffnete Reihe,
> Doppelreihe,
> Keil (Bild 6),
> Geöffnete Linie.

77. Bewegungen und Formveränderungen des leichten Zuges werden nach den in den Ziffern 44 bis 54 gegebenen Grundsätzen sinngemäß ausgeführt.

78. Die „Linie" kann als Versammlungsform befohlen werden. Aufmärsche aus der Bewegung zur Linie sind nicht zu üben.

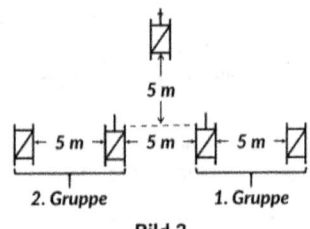

Bild 3
Der „Zug in Linie".

1. Formations and Movements.

76. Formations of the platoon are:

Assembly formations

    line (Figure 3),

    column (Figure 4);

marching formations

    column,

    double column (Figure 5);

combat formations

    open column,

    double column,

    wedge (Figure 6),

    open line.

77. Movements and formation changes of the light platoon are carried out in accordance with the principles set out in Numbers 44 to 54.

78. The "line" may be ordered as a formation of assembly. Assembly from movement to line are not to be practiced.

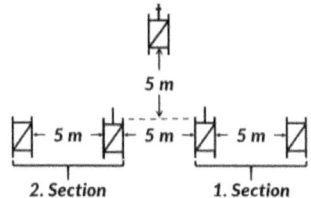

Figure 3
The "platoon in line".

79. Die „Reihe" ist die gebräuchlichste Marsch- und Versammlungsform. Sie ist zugleich die Marschordnung des Zuges auf der Straße. Der Abstand von Fahrzeug zu Fahrzeug beträgt in der Versammlung etwa 5 m, während der Fahrt etwa 25 m. Über Abstände beim „Halt" vgl. Ziffer 54.

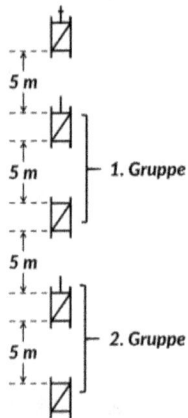

Bild 4
Der Zug „in Reihe" (Versammlungsform).

80. Die „Doppelreihe" ist die gebräuchlichste Form für den entfalteten Marsch des Zuges. Der Abstand von Fahrzeug zu Fahrzeug beträgt etwa 25 m, der Zwischenraum der beiden Gruppen in der Regel 50 m; er richtet sich beim entfalteten Vorgehen auf dem Gefechtsfeld nach Gelände und Feindeinwirkung.

79. The "column" is the most common formation for march and assembly. It is also the march order of the platoon on the street. The distance from vehicle to vehicle is about 5 m during assembly and about 25 m when moving. For distances at "stop" see Number 54[87].

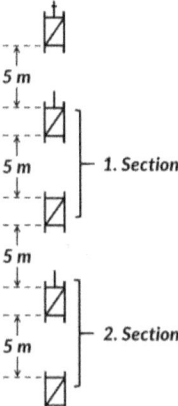

Figure 4
The platoon "in column" (assembly formation).

80. The "double column" is the most common formation for the march in preliminary deployment[88] of the platoon. The clearance between two vehicles is about 25 m, while the distance between the two sections is usually 50 m; this depends on the terrain and the enemy action during the advance in preliminary deployment on the battlefield.

---

[87] Go to Number 54.

[88] Since we translated "Entfaltung" with "preliminary deployment" the translation of "entfalteten" is a bit a cumbersome, since in this instance it is not used as a noun. For further information see the Section "A Note on the Use of 'Deployment' [...]" in Supplement 2.

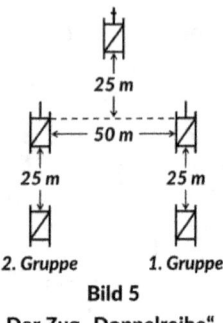

Bild 5
Der Zug „Doppelreihe".

81. Der „Keil" ist die gebräuchlichste Angriffsform des Zuges. Der Zwischenraum von Fahrzeug zu Fahrzeug beträgt etwa 50 m; Abstand in der Regel 25 m.

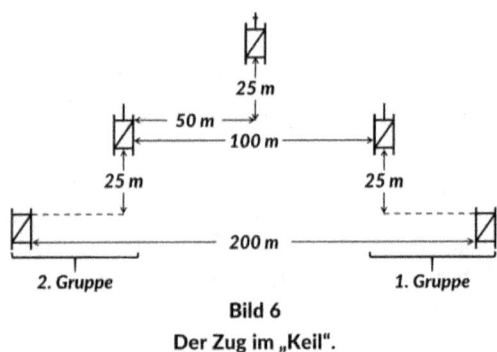

Bild 6
Der Zug im „Keil".

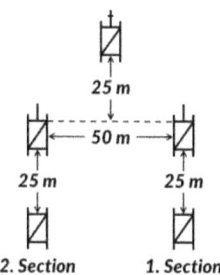

Figure 5
The platoon in "double column".

81. The "wedge" is the most common attack formation of the platoon. The distance from vehicle to vehicle is about 50 m; clearance is usually 25 m.

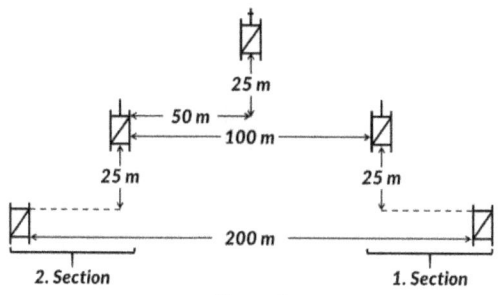

Figure 6
The platoon in the "wedge".

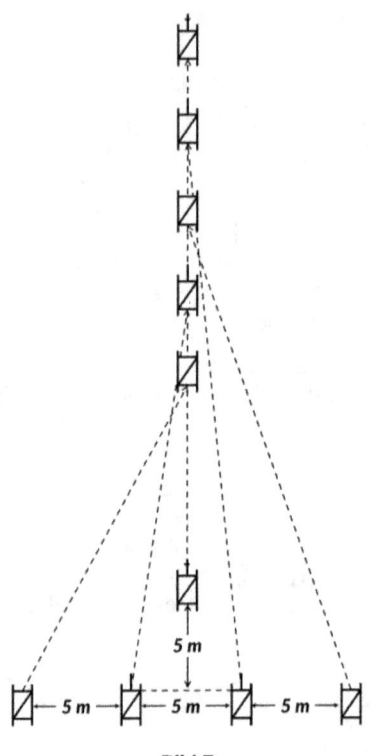

Bild 7
Formveränderung aus „Linie" zur „Reihe".

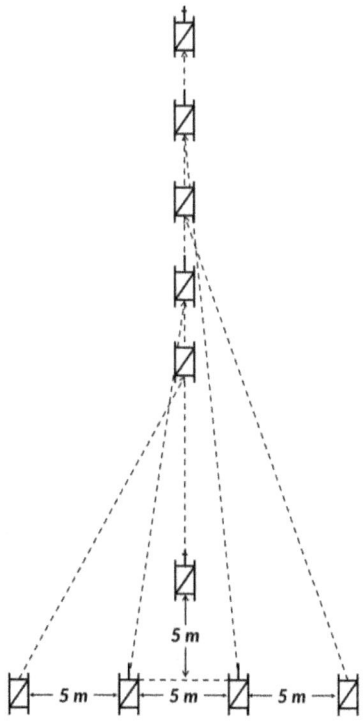

Figure 7
Change of formation from "line" to "column".

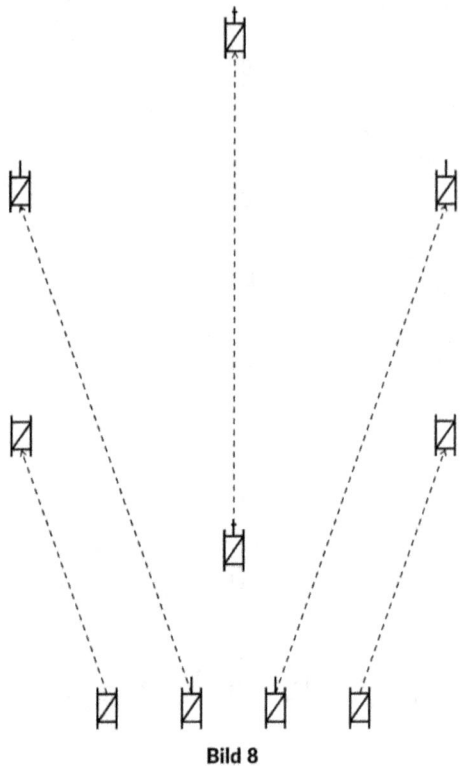

Bild 8
Formveränderung aus „Linie" zur „Doppelreihe".

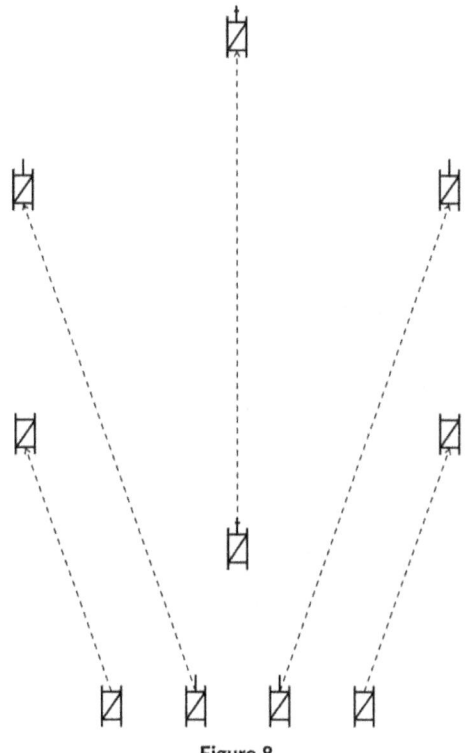

Figure 8

Change of formation from "line" to "double column".

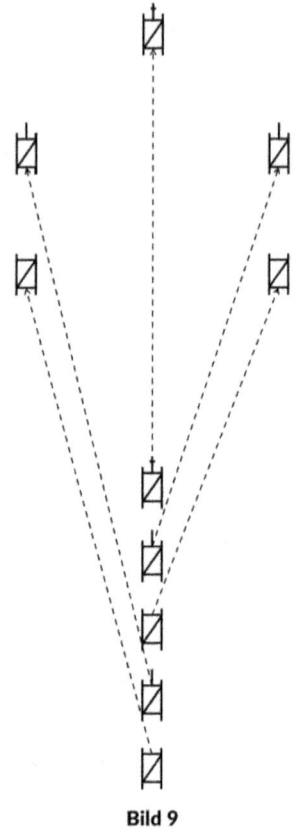

Bild 9
Formveränderung aus „Reihe" zur „Doppelreihe".

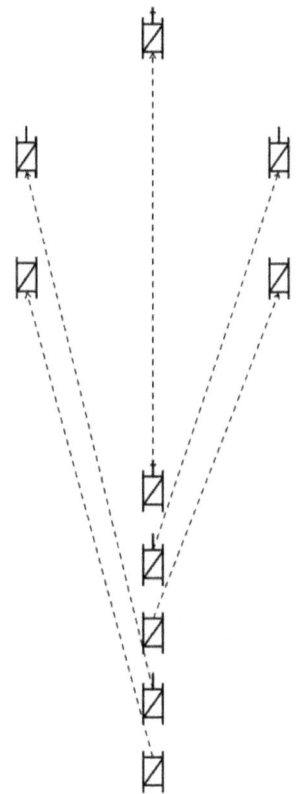

Figure 9
Change of formation from "column" to "double column".

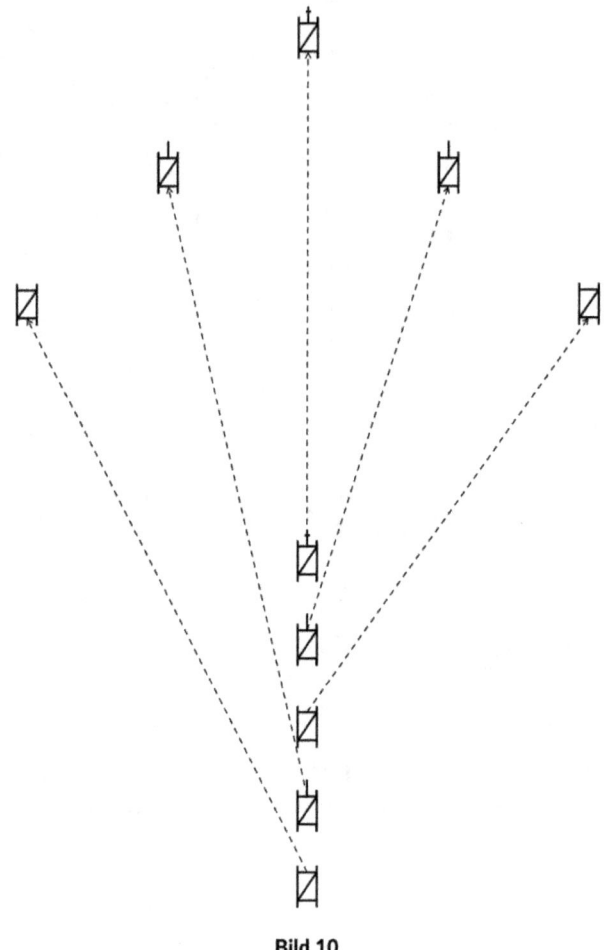

Bild 10
Formveränderung aus „Reihe" zum „Keil".

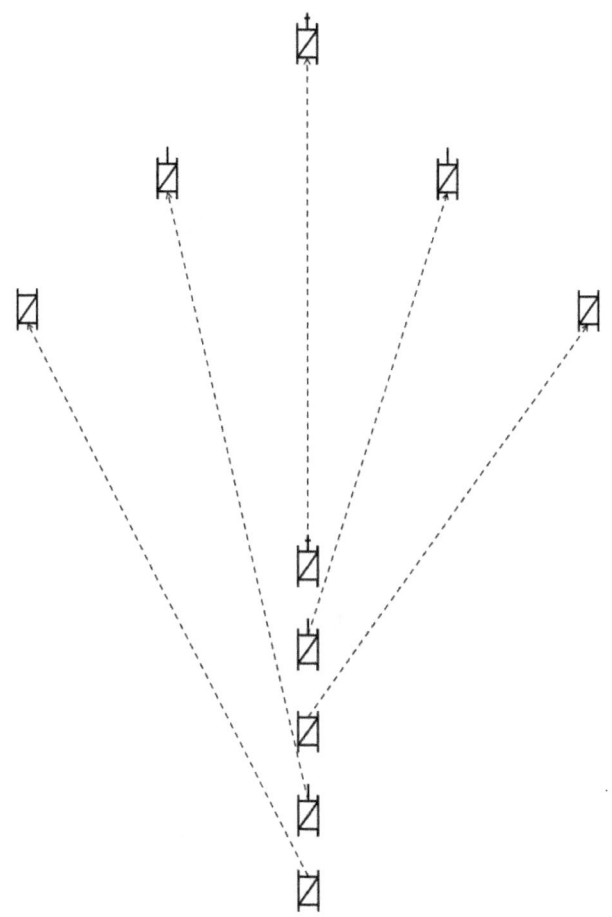

Figure 10
Change of formation from "column" to "wedge".

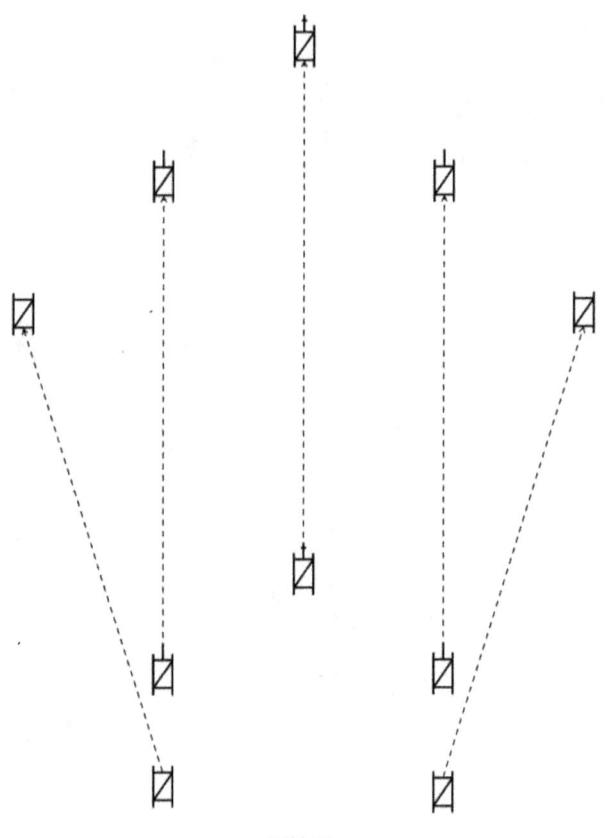

Bild 11
Formveränderung aus „Doppelreihe" zum „Keil".

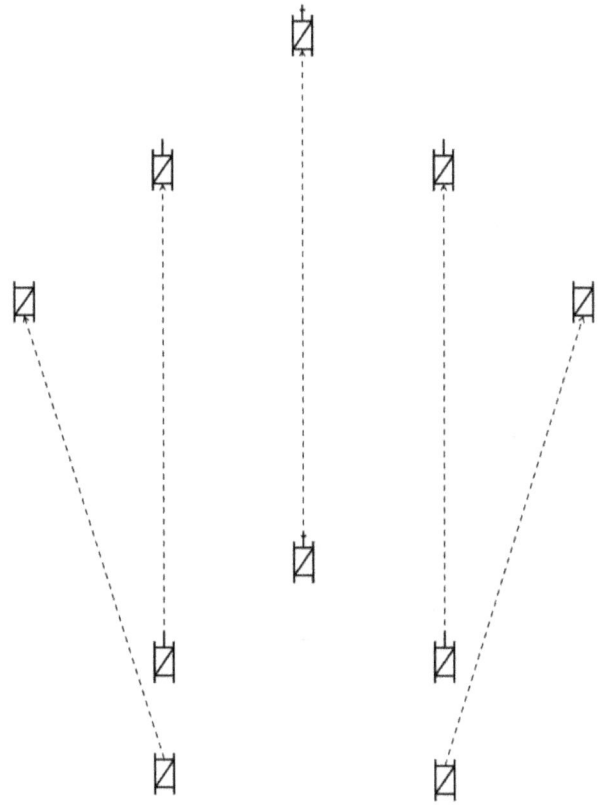

Figure 11
Change of formation from "double column" to "wedge".

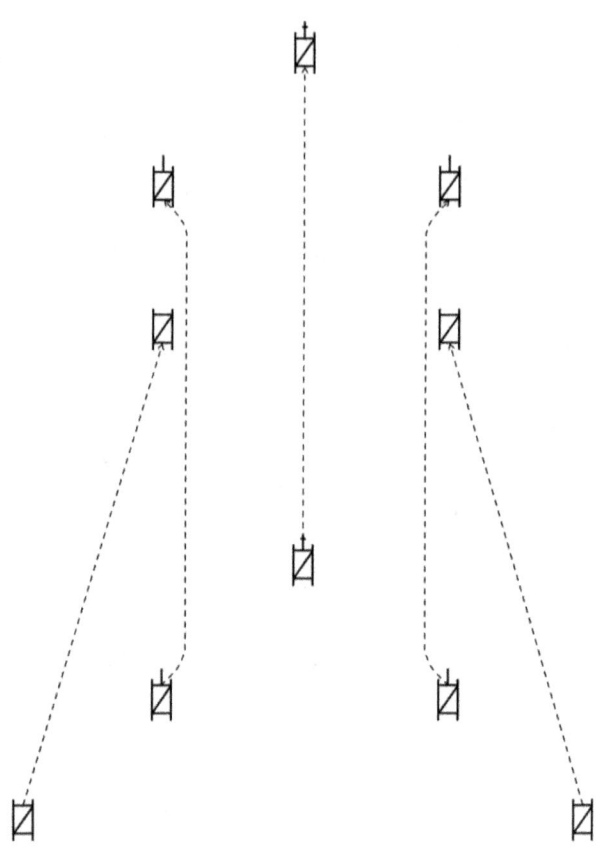

Bild 12
Formveränderung aus „Keil" zur „Doppelreihe".

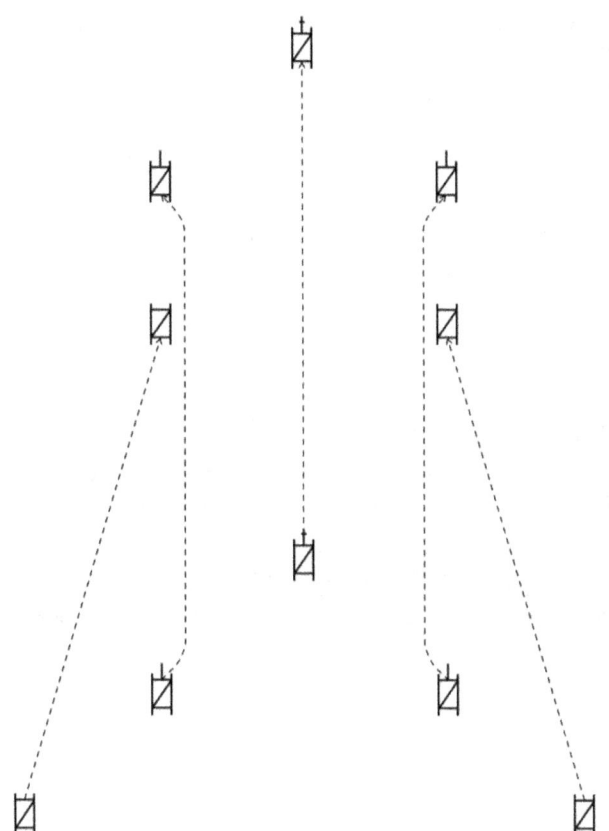

Figure 12
Change of formation from "wedge" to "double column".

2. Der leichte Zug im Gefecht.

82. Wichtigste Aufgaben des leichten Zuges sind **Aufklärung, Sicherung** und **Verbindung**.

Daneben übernimmt er oft Kampfaufträge im Rahmen der Kompanie, häufig den Schutz des Kompanie-Trupps[89].

83. Die Gefechtsaufklärung setzt ein, sobald Fühlung mit dem Feind genommen ist. Sie hat den Zweck:

> Einzelheiten über den Feind festzustellen, insbesondere
>> seine Flügel und Flanken,
>>
>> die Richtung, in der er sich bewegt,
>>
>> seine Stärke;
>
> die eigenen Panzerkampfwagen bei Entfaltung und Entwicklung vor Überraschung zu schützen;
>
> vor der angreifenden Kompanie die feindlichen Abwehrwaffen sowie Hindernisse und Sperren frühzeitig zu erkennen.

84. Zur Erfüllung dieser Aufgabe geht der Zug auseinandergezogen und in Gruppen aufgelöst sprungweise über gute Beobachtungspunkte vor.

Die Gruppen sollen viel sehen, aber nicht gesehen werden; sie sollen aufklären, in der Regel aber nicht kämpfen.

---

[89] Anmerkung: Sonst wurde „Kompanietrupp" nicht „Kompanie-Trupp" geschrieben.

2. The Light Platoon in an Engagement.

82. The most important tasks of the light platoon are **reconnaissance**, **security** and **communication**.

Besides this it frequently performs combat missions on the company level, such as the protection of the company headquarters section[90].

83. Combat reconnaissance begins as soon as contact with the enemy is made. It has the purpose:

> to gain information about the enemy, in particular
>> his wings and flanks,
>>
>> the direction of his movement,
>>
>> his strength;
>
> to protect friendly tanks from surprises during preliminary deployment and full deployment[91];
>
> to detect, in a timely manner, enemy defensive weapons as well as obstacles and barriers before the attacking company.

84. To fulfil this task, the platoon is spread-out and divided into sections and advances by bounds between good observation positions.

The sections should see much, but not be seen; as a rule they should scout, not fight.

---

[90] Translation notice with the exception of this instance, the H. Dv. always used to combined word of "Kompanietrupp" instead of "Kompanie-Trupp". The meaning does not change.

[91] "Entfaltung" literally translated is "unfolding". Yet, we translated it with "preliminary deployment" according to Condell and Zabecki. Previously, the US Army 1944 translation had been "development". This has changed as in modern usage, "developing" happens at a later stage. Similarly, "Entwicklung" literally translated is "development", meaning "full deployment". This translation uses the latter term to make a clearer distinction to "preliminary development". For further information see the Section "A Note on the Use of 'Deployment' [...]" in Supplement 2.

85. Der leichte Zug kämpft nur

> zur Selbstverteidigung bei feindlichem Angriff, vor allem durch Panzerjäger und Panzerkampfwagen,
>
> zur Beseitigung von Hindernissen und Sperren, die nicht umfahren werden können,
>
> zur Ausnutzung besonders günstiger Gelegenheiten, wenn er hierdurch von seiner Aufgabe nicht abgelenkt wird.

86. Alle Aufklärungsergebnisse und wichtigen Beobachtungen sind dem übergeordneten Führer sofort zu melden.

87. Gefechtsaufklärung vor der Front der angreifenden Kompanie erfordert Feuerschutz. Kann er infolge der räumlichen Entfernung weder durch die Kompanie, noch durch andere Kräfte gegeben werden, unterstützen sich die Gruppen beim Vorgehen wechselseitig durch Feuer.

88. Erfordert die Feindlage, die Feuerkraft im Zuge zusammenzuhalten, wird die entsprechende Gefechtsform nach Ziff. 76 eingenommen.

89. Verstärkt sich der feindliche Widerstand, vor allem die Abwehr durch panzerbrechende Waffen, läßt sich der leichte Zug durch seine Kompanie aufnehmen.

85. The light platoon only fights

> for self-defense if attacked by the enemy, especially by anti-tank units[92] and tanks,
>
> to remove obstacles and barriers that cannot be bypassed,
>
> to take advantage of particularly favorable opportunities if they do not distract the platoon from its task.

86. All reconnaissance results and important observations are to be reported immediately to the superior commander.

87. Combat reconnaissance in front of the attacking company requires protective fire. If it cannot be provided by the company due to the spatial distance, nor be provided by other forces, the sections support each other with fire while advancing.

88. If the enemy position requires the concentration of firepower the corresponding combat formation shall be adopted in accordance with No. 76[93].

89. If the enemy resistance, above all the defense by armor-piercing weapons, increases, the light platoon is reintegrated into its company.

---

[92] "Panzerjäger" literally means "tank hunter", which was both the general name of the anti-tank units since 1940 and vehicles like the "Panzerjäger I". In this case it refers to anti-tank units.

[93] Go to Number 76.

90. Beim Einbruch in die feindliche Stellung setzt er sich hinter die vordersten mittleren Züge. Erst nach erfolgtem Durchbruch übernimmt er wieder die Aufklärung vor der Front.

91. Ist der Zug zur Sicherung des Marsches eingesetzt, so ist es seine Aufgabe, die Kompanie vor überraschendem Angriff zu schützen. Schwächeren Widerstand bricht er selbstständig und stellt so die rasche Vorwärtsbewegung der ihm folgenden Einheit sicher.

92. Als **Sicherung** in der **Bereitstellung** und bei Rasten ist der Zug so einzusetzen, daß er

> a) bei **Tage** den Raum, in dem sich der Feind nähern kann, von gedeckten Übersichtspunkten aus lückenlos beherrscht;

> b) bei **Nacht** in enger Anlehnung an Straßen und Ortschaften die Anmarschwege unter Feuer nehmen kann.

93. Die Verbindung mit der zu sichernden Einheit ist stets aufrechtzuerhalten.

94. Sicherungen sind zweckmäßig durch Kradfahrer[94] zu verstärken.

---

[94] Krad ist die Kurzform von Kraftrad, eine alte Bezeichnung für Motorrad. Ein schweres Krad ist ein Motorrad mit Beiwagen.

90. When breaking into the enemy position, it [the light platoon] is positioned behind the foremost medium platoons. Only after a successful penetration does it resume reconnaissance forward of the front line.

91. If the platoon is used to secure the march, its task is to protect the company from surprise attack. Weaker resistance is to be crushed independently and thus ensures the rapid forward movement of the following units.

92. The platoon is to be used for **security** in the **assembly areas** and during rest in such a way that

> a) during **daytime,** it controls from covered viewpoints the area from which the enemy may approach;
>
> b) at **nighttime** it, in close relation to roads and settlements, can cover the approach routes with fire.

93. The communication with the covered unit is to be maintained at all times.

94. Protective measures are to be appropriately reinforced with motorcyclists[95].

---

[95] The German original refers to "Kradfahrer". This is an old composite word, combining "Krad" as the short form of "Kraftrad" (literally "force/power bike", which is an old term for motorcycle) with "Fahrer" (driver). A "heavy Krad" is a motorcycle with a sidecar.

E. Die Kompanie.

I. Allgemeines.

95. Von den beiden im Kompanietrupp befindlichen Panzerkampfwagen IV dient ein Wagen als Führer-, der andere als Reservefahrzeug.

Die im Kompanietrupp befindlichen 3 Kradmelder dienen zur Befehlsübermittlung. Bei Gefechtsbeginn treten sie mit dem Pkw. des Kompanieführers zum Gefechtstroß I.

96. Der **Gefechtstroß** wird in Gefechtstroß I und II eingeteilt.

Der **Gefechtstroß I** ist klein zu halten. Seine Zusammensetzung wechselt und muß den Erfordernissen des Kampfes angepaßt sein.

Zum Gefechtstroß I können gehören:

    Betriebsstoffwagen,

    Munitionswagen,

    Gerätewagen für Waffenmeistergerät,

    Teile der Wechselbesatzung (Reservefahrer),

    Feldküche.

Er wird von einem älteren Unteroffizier[96] geführt.

---

[96] Anmerkung: Unteroffizier war sowohl ein Rang, als auch eine Kategorie von Soldaten, die nicht zu den Mannschaften oder Offizieren gehören.

E. The Company.
I. General Information.

95. Of the two Panzerkampfwagen IV in the company headquarters section, one serves as the commander's vehicle, the other as a reserve vehicle.

The 3 motorcycle messengers in the company headquarters section are used for the dispatch of orders. At the beginning of an engagement, they join the combat train I with the car from the company commander.

96. The **combat trains** are divided into combat train I and II.

The **combat trains I** are to be kept small. Its composition changes and must be adapted to combat requirements.

Combat train I may include:

> fuel vehicle,
>
> ammunition vehicle,
>
> equipment vehicle for armorer-artificer equipment,
>
> parts of the replacement crew[97] (reserve drivers),
>
> field kitchen.

It is led by an older NCO[98].

---

[97] The literal translation of the German word "Wechselbesatzung" would be "change crew". Meant are crew members that can be exchanged when needed to relieve, substitute or reinforce the existing crews.

[98] Note: "Unteroffizier" was both a rank and a category of soldier, namely non-commissioned officer (NCO), so all personal who were not enlisted men nor officers.

97. Zum **Gefechtstroß II** gehören alle übrigen Fahrzeuge sowie die restlichen Teile der Wechselbesatzung.

Er wird meist vom Hauptfeldwebel[99] geführt.

98. Der Gefechtstroß I der Kompanien wird während des Gefechts zusammengefaßt und von einem Offizier nach Anordnung der Abteilung oder des Regiments nachgeführt.

99. Der Gefechtstroß II sämtlicher Kompanien wird von der Abteilung während des Marsches und während des Gefechts zusammengefaßt und unter einem Offizier nach Anordnung der Abteilung oder des Regiments nachgeführt.

100. Die **Instandsetzungsgruppe** befindet sich meist bei der Kampfstaffel. Wird die Abteilung geschlossen eingesetzt, trifft sie zum Abteilungs-Ingenieur-Offizier.

101. Der **Sanitätstrupp** tritt während des Gefechts zum Abteilungsarzt.

102. Der **Gepäcktroß** wird innerhalb der Abteilung zusammengefaßt und in der Regel verbandsweise (z. B. von der Division) bewegt.

---

[99] Hauptfeldwebel oft auch „Spieß" oder „Mutter der Kompanie" war kein Rang, sondern ein Posten. Seine Aufgabe war die Entlastung des Kompanieführers von Aufgaben, die nichts mit dem Kampf zu tun hatten.

97. Combat train II includes all other vehicles and the remaining parts of the replacement crew.

It is usually led by the company sergeant major[100].

98. Combat train I of the companies are collected during the engagement and follow the battalion or regiment with an officer after receiving the order.

99. Combat train II of all companies are assembled by the battalion during march and engagements and are commanded by an officer following battalion or regimental orders.

100. The **maintenance section** is mostly located at the combat echelon. If the battalion is committed as a whole, it is assigned to the battalion's maintenance officer[101].

101. The **medical team** is assigned to the battalion's doctor during an engagement.

102. The **baggage trains** are grouped together within the battalion and are usually moved within a larger formation[102] (e.g. by the division).

---

[100] In the Wehrmacht, the company sergeant major, often with varying affection referred to as "Spieß" (literally "skewer") or "mother of the company", was not a rank but an appointment. His task was to relieve the company commander of non-combat related tasks.

[101] From the German original of "Abteilungs-Ingenieur-Offizier".

[102] The German original uses the word "Verbandsweise" which presents a complicated term, since a "Verband" could be a union of units, but also a larger formation capable of combined arms warfare usually a brigade or division. "Verbandsweise" literally is "formation-wise".

II. Formen und Bewegungen.

103. Ohne Fahrzeuge tritt die Kompanie auf das Kommando: **„In Linie – angetreten!"** in der Gliederung:

    Kampfstaffel,

    Räderstaffel an.

Die Kampfstaffel ist untergliedert in:

    Kompanietrupp,

    Leichter Zug,

    1. bis 3. Zug,

    Wechselbesatzung.

Innerhalb der Räderstaffel:

    Kompanietrupp,

    Staffel für Wechselbesatzungen,

    Gefechtstroß,

    Instandsetzungsgruppe,

    Gepäcktroß.

Der Hauptfeldwebel steht am rechten Flügel der Räderstaffel, der Schirrmeister (als Schließender) mit dem Sanitätsdienstgrad am linken.

Gewehrträger stehen mit Gewehr ab.

II. Formations and Movements.

103. Without vehicles the company falls in on the command: **"In line – fall in"** in the composition:

    combat echelon,

    wheel echelon.

The combat element is subdivided into:

    company headquarters section,

    light platoon,

    1st to 3rd platoon,

    replacement crew.

Within the wheeled vehicle element:

    company headquarters section,

    echelon for replacement crews,

    combat train,

    maintenance section,

    baggage train.

The company sergeant major stands on the right wing of the wheel echelon, the maintenance technical sergeant (as closer) with the acting medical personnel on the left.

Rifle bearers stand with rifles set at ease.

104. Auf das Kommando: **„An die – Fahrzeuge!"** begibt sich die Kompanie auf die Plätze an den Fahrzeugen. Die Kampfstaffel tritt an den Fahrzeugen nach H. Dv. 470/5b[103] und 5d an. Die Wechselbesatzung und Mannschaften des Gefechtstrosses treten hinter ihren Fahrzeugen an, die übrigen Besatzungen auf ihren Plätzen am Fahrzeug. Die Gewehre werden auf dem Wege zum Fahrzeug von den Kradfahrern umgehängt.

Auf das Kommando: **„Gerät an die Fahrzeuge!"** bringen die Kradfahrer und Begleiter Gewehre und Brotbeutel im Fahrzeug unter.

105. Soll der Motor mit Schwungkraftanlasser angelassen werden, so ist es zu befehlen.

106. Wird **„Aufsitzen!"** ohne das Kommando „An die – Fahrzeuge!" befohlen, so begibt sich alles im Laufschritt an die Fahrzeuge, macht sich zum Aufsitzen fertig und sitzt nach H. Dv. 470/5b[104] bzw. 5d auf.

107. Beim **Absitzen** ist für die Wechselbesatzungen und den Gefechtstroß das Absitzen besonders zu befehlen.

108. Soll nach dem Absitzen mit Gerät angetreten werden, so ist zu befehlen: **„Gerät umhängen!"**.

---

[103] Siehe Ergänzung 1 im Anhang für den vollständigen Titel.
[104] Siehe Ergänzung 1 im Anhang für den vollständigen Titel.

104. On the command: **"To the - vehicles!"** the company assumes their positions in the vehicles. The combat element falls in with the vehicles according to H. Dv. 470/5b[105] and 5d. The replacement crews[106] and the crews of the combat trains fall in behind their vehicles, the other crews assume their places on the vehicle. On their way to the vehicle, the rifles are slung on by the motorcyclists.

On the command: **"Equipment to the vehicles!"** the motorcyclists and companions store rifles and bread bags in the vehicle.

105. If the engine is to be started with an inertia starter, a command will be given.

106. If the command "**Mount**"! is given without the command "To the vehicles", everyone will move at a run to the vehicles, and gets ready to mount according to H. Dv. 470/5b[107] or 5d.

107. When **dismounting,** a specific order is given to the auxiliary crews and the combat trains.

108. If after dismounting, the unit is to fall in with their equipment, the order: **"Sling on equipment!"** will be given.

---

[105] See Supplement 1 in the Appendix for the full title.

[106] See explanation in the footnote of Number 96.

[107] See Supplement 1 in the Appendix for the full title.

109. Formen der Kampfstaffel sind:

In der Versammlung:
> Linie (Bild 1),
> Kompaniekolonne (Bild 2),
> Reihe,
> Doppelreihe (Bild 3).

Beim Marsch:
> Reihe,
> Doppelreihe.

Im Gefecht:
> Geöffnete Reihe,
> Doppelreihe,
> Geöffnete Linie (Bild 4),
> Keil (Bild 5),
> Breitkeil (Bild 6).

Die Gefechtsformen gelten für den geschlossenen Einsatz der Kompanie.

110. Bei Aufmärschen fährt der an zweiter Stelle fahrende Zug *rechts*, der an dritter Stelle fahrende Zug *links* auf.

111. Der in der Mitte fahrende Zug hat meist **Richtung** und **Anschluß**[108]. Soll auf einen anderen Zug Anschluß genommen werden, so ist dies zu befehlen.

112. Soll bei Formveränderungen zum Aufmarschieren oder Abbrechen ein anderer Zug Richtung und Anschluß haben, muß dies befohlen werden.

---

[108] Bzgl. Anschluß siehe Glossar.

109. The formations of the combat element are:

At assembly:
> line (Figure 1),
>
> company column (Figure 2),
>
> column,
>
> double column (Figure 3).

During march:
> column,
>
> double column.

During engagement:
> open column,
>
> double column,
>
> open line (Figure 4),
>
> wedge (Figure 5),
>
> inverted wedge (Figure 6).

The combat formations apply if the company is employed as a whole unit[109].

110. During assembly, the platoon driving in the second position drives on the *right*, the platoon driving in the third position drives on the *left*.

111. The platoon driving in the middle usually gives **direction** and **contact**[110]. If contact is to be made to another platoon, this is to be ordered.

112. If during formation changes for assembly or breaking off a different platoon should have direction and contact, this must be ordered.

---

[109] See Glossary: Employment of the Whole Unit (Einsatz, geschlossen).

[110] From the German "Anschluß", which in this case is translated with "contact". It refers to a person, vehicle or unit which was used as a reference point. For further information see the Glossary.

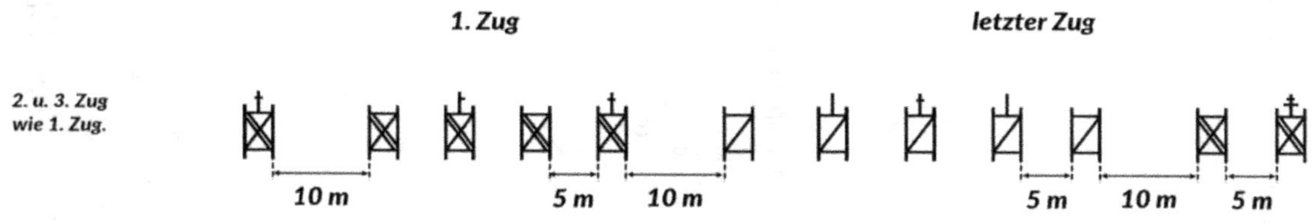

2. u. 3. Zug
wie 1. Zug.

1. Zug

letzter Zug

10 m   5 m   10 m   5 m   10 m   5 m

Bild 1
Kampfstaffel in „Linie".

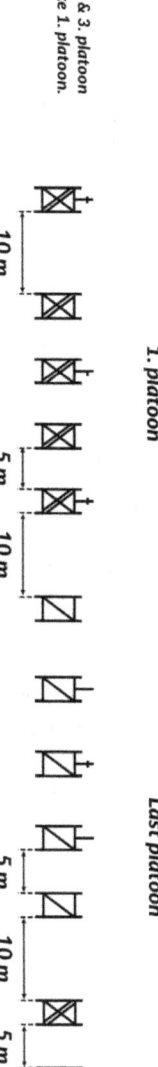

Figure 1
Combat elements in "line".

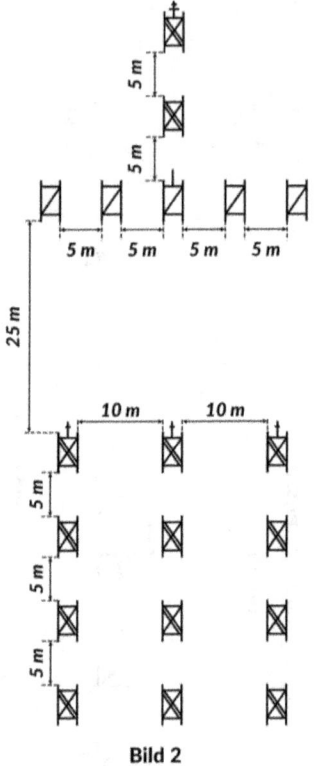

Bild 2
Kampfstaffel in „Kompaniekolonne".

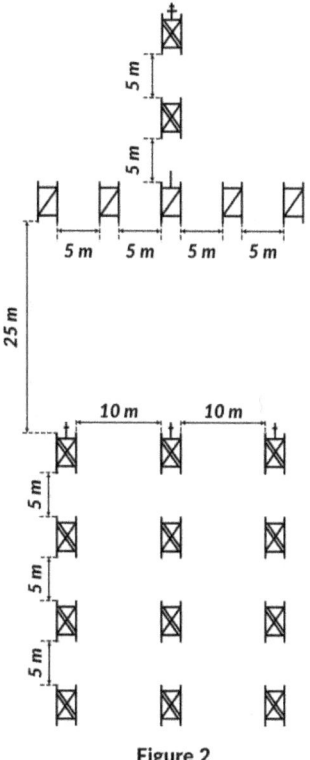

Figure 2

Combat elements in "company column".

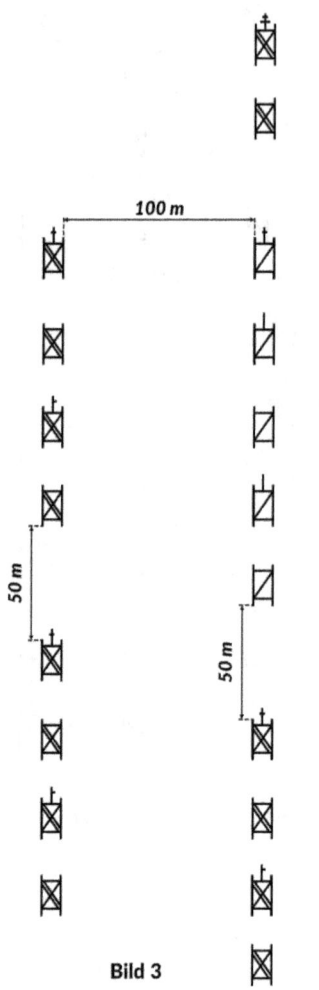

Bild 3
Kampfstaffel in „Doppelreihe" (Versammlungsform).

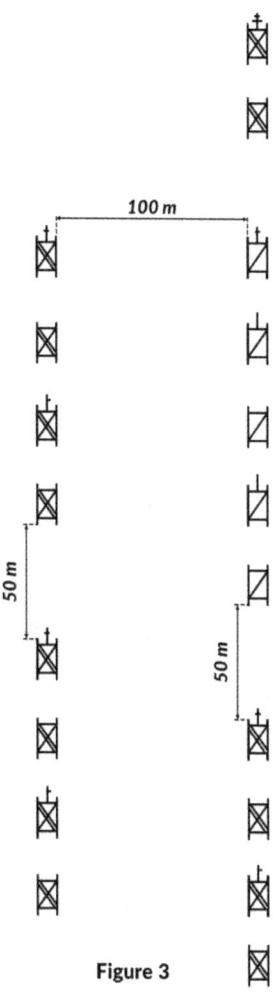

Figure 3
Combat elements in "double column" (assembly formation).

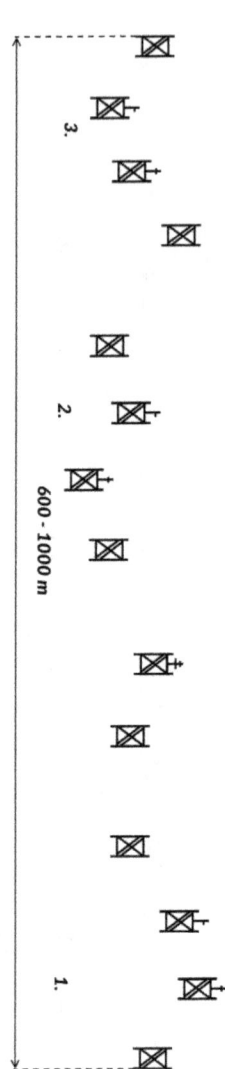

Bild 4
Beispiel für die geöffnete „Linie" (leichter Zug des Kompanietrupps nicht dargestellt).

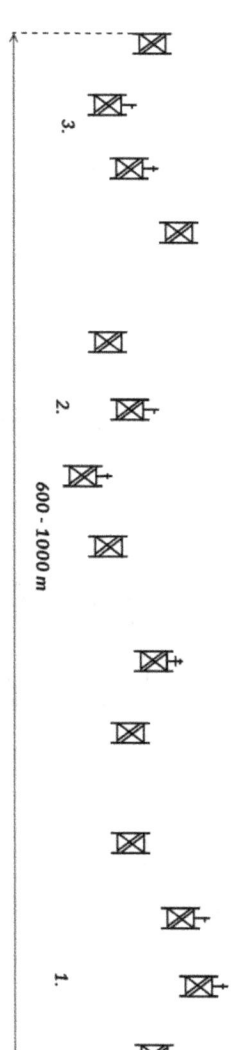

Figure 4
Example for the opened "line" (light platoon of the company headquarters not shown).

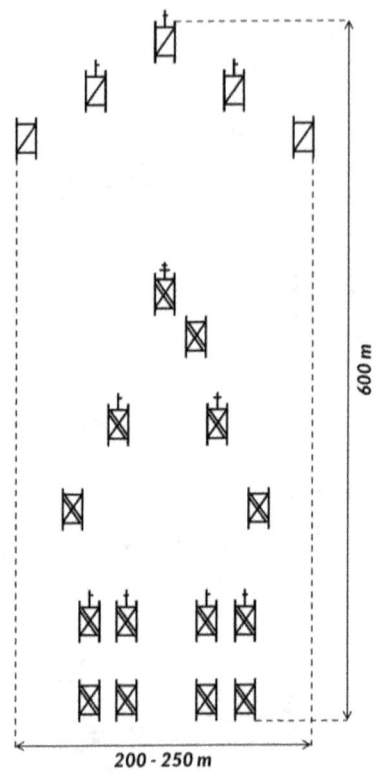

Bild 5
Kampfstaffel in „Keil".

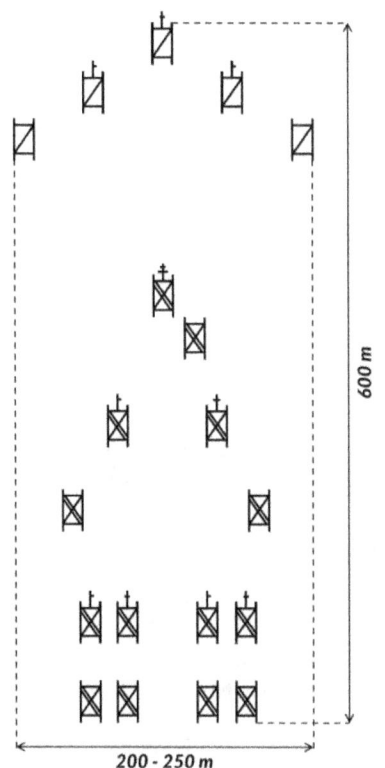

Figure 5
Combat elements in "wedge".

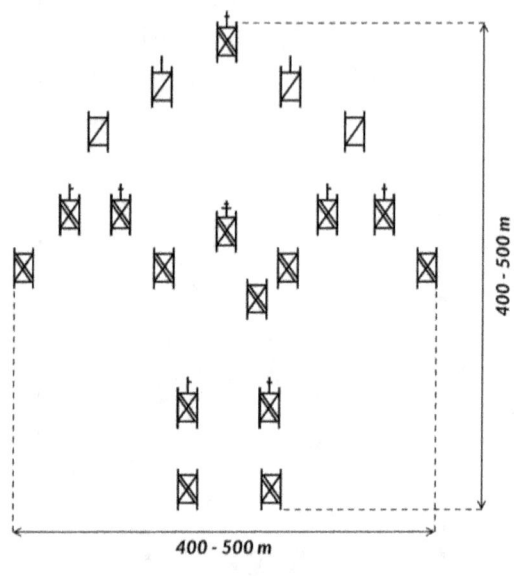

Bild 6
Kampfstaffel im „Breitkeil".

III. Führung.

113. Der Kompanieführer fährt so lange vor seiner Kompanie, bis die vorderen Züge den Kampf aufgenommen haben. Dann führt er von dem Platz, der die beste Beobachtung des Gefechtsfeldes gestattet. Ist die Kompanie in zweiter Linie eingesetzt, bleibt er vor seiner Kompanie.

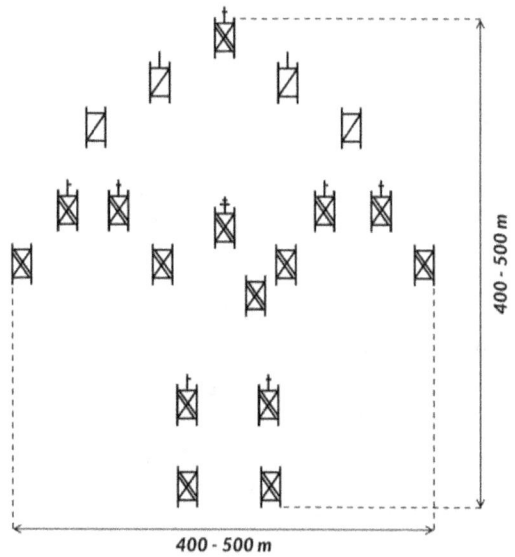

Figure 6

Combat elements in "inverted wedge".

III. Command.

113. The company commander drives in front of his company until the front platoons have taken up the fight. Then he leads from a position that affords the best observation of the battlefield. If the company is second in line, he stays in front of his company.

114. Sind Züge den leichten Kompanie unterstellt, fährt er mit dem Rest der Kompanie zur Verfügung der Abteilung nach deren Befehl.

IV. Marsch und Gefecht.

a) Marsch.

115. Marschiert die Kompanie **allein**, folgen die Radfahrzeuge der Kampfstaffel sprungweise.

Ist nicht mit Feindberührung zu rechnen, kann die Räderstaffel mit Ausnahme der Instandsetzungsgruppe und des Betriebsstoffwagen auch bis zum nächsten Halt vorausgeschickt werden.

116. Marschiert die Kompanie im **Verbande der Abteilung**, werden Kampfstaffeln und Räderstaffeln aller Kompanien meist in zwei getrennten Marschgruppen durch die Abteilung geführt.

Bei der Kampfstaffel fahren Pkw. des Kompanieführers, Kradmelder, J-Gruppe[111] und Sanitätstrupp.

117. Der Kompanieführer fährt mit dem Kompanietrupp am Anfang der Kompanie. Am Ende fahren als Schließende der Schirrmeister mit einem Kradmelder und der Sanitätsdienstgrad.

118. Ist mit **Feindberührung** zu rechnen und marschiert die Kompanie allein, sichert der leichte Zug verstärkt durch einen Halbzug und Kradfahrer die Stetigkeit des Marsches.

119. Während des Marsches wird gerührt. Richtschützen, Ladeschützen und Funker können sich in die

---

[111] Hierbei handelt es sich um die Instandsetzungsgruppe. Das „J" am Anfang des Wortes wurde im Heer bzw. generell in der Vergangenheit häufig genutzt statt dem „I" (i), z.B.: Infanteriegeschütz wurde meist mit J. G. abgekürzt. Dies hat zum Teil historische und zum Teil praktische Gründe, da es in gewissen Schriftarten zu Verwechslungen zwischen dem kleinen „L" und großen „i" kommen kann.

114. If platoons are subordinated to the light company, he [company commander] remains with the rest of the company and remains at the disposal of the battalion under its command.

IV. March and Engagement.

a) March.

115. If the company marches **alone**, the wheeled vehicles follow the combat element while advancing by bounds.

If no contact with the enemy is to be expected, the wheel echelon can also be sent ahead until the next stop, with the exception of the maintenance section and the fuel vehicle.

116. If the company marches in **unity with the battalion**, combat element and wheeled vehicle element of all companies are usually led by the battalion in two separate march-groups.

The cars of the company commander, the motorcycle messengers, the maintenance section [J-section[112]] and medical team drive with the combat element.

117. The company commander is driving with the company headquarters section at the front of the company. The master technical sergeant with a motorcyclist messenger and the medical NCO drive at the end as the closing element.

118. If **contact with the enemy** is to be expected and the company marches alone, the light platoon secures, reinforced by a half-platoon and motorcyclists, the steadiness of the march.

119. During the march [the men are] at ease. Gunners, loaders and radio operators can

---

[112] This is the maintenance section. The "J" at the beginning of the word was often used in the German Army or in general in the past instead of the "I" (i), for example: Infantry guns were usually abbreviated J. G. This has historical and practical reasons, because in some fonts it can lead to confusions between the small "L" with the large "i".

Luken des Panzers setzen. Sitzen auf Panzeraufbau während der Fahrt ist verboten.

Marscherleichterungen, wie Ausziehen der Feldjacke, Hochschlagen der Ärmel sind innerhalb der Kompanie einheitlich zu befehlen.

120. Der **Marschbefehl** muß enthalten:

Feindlage,

Marschziel,

Marschweg,

Abmarschplatz,

Abmarschzeit,

Gliederung auf dem Marsch,

Sicherung,

Verkehrsregelung,

Besondere Anordnungen (Versorgung mit Betriebsstoff und Verpflegung, Beleuchtungsstufe, Funkbereitschaft, Gefechtsbereitschaft, Marscherleichterungen),

Halte und Rasten,

Verhalten zurückbleibende Fahrzeuge,

Platz des Führers.

121. Halte und **Rasten** sind so zu wählen, daß das Freimachen der Marschstraße sichergestellt ist. Je nach Gelände sind zur Schonung von Material und Besatzung Halte – der erste spätestens nach 1 Stunde – einzulegen.

Für Rasten mit Verpflegung und Betriebsstoffausgabe sind im allgemeinen 3 bis 4 Stunden anzusetzen.

sit in the open hatches of the tank. It is forbidden to sit on the tank turret and hull while driving.

Marching conveniences, such as taking off the field jacket or raising the sleeves are to be ordered uniformly within the company.

120. The **marching orders** must contain:

>enemy situation,
>
>march destination,
>
>marching route,
>
>point of departure,
>
>time to move out,
>
>march composition,
>
>security,
>
>traffic regulations,
>
>special arrangements (supply of fuel and food, lighting level, radio readiness, combat readiness, marching conveniences),
>
>stops and rests,
>
>behavior of remaining vehicles,
>
>position of the commander.

121. Stops and **rests** are chosen so as to ensure that the marching road is cleared. Depending on the terrain, stops must be made to preserve the material and crew with the first to be made after 1 hour at the latest.

For rests with food and fuel, 3 to 4 hours should be scheduled.

Während der Halte und Rasten haben die Panzerfahrer, erforderlichenfalls unter Mithilfe der Panzerwarte die Fahrzeuge zu überprüfen und kleine Instandsetzungen auszuführen.

b) Entfaltung.

122. Die Kompanie entfaltet sich, wenn die Feindwirkung durch Flieger und Artillerie den Marsch in einer Kolonne verbietet, oder vor einem Aufmarsch zum Gefecht. Sie nimmt in der Entfaltung die Form ein, die günstige Voraussetzungen für den Kampf schafft.

Die Entfaltung wird meist in der Bewegung durchgeführt.

123. Den Befehl zur Entfaltung gibt in der Regel der Abteilungs- oder Regimentsführer. Zwingt die Feindlage zu schneller Entfaltung, z.B. bei plötzlichem Zusammentreffen mit dem Feind, wird sie vom Kompanieführer befohlen.

c) Angriff.

124. Die **Stärke des Angriffs** der mittleren Kompanie liegt im **geschlossenen Einsatz**.

Hierzu sind jedoch in der Regel Vorbedingung:

    Übersichtlichkeit des Geländes,

    Überhöhende Feuerstellungen,

    Angriffsbreite der Abteilung nicht über 1200 m.

During stops and rests the tank drivers must inspect the vehicles and if necessary, with the assistance of the tank maintenance crews, carry out minor repairs,

b) Preliminary Deployment[113].

122. The company performs a preliminary deployment when the threat[114] of enemy aircraft and artillery prohibits the march in a column, or before the assembly for an engagement. During the preliminary deployment it moves into the formation that creates favorable preconditions for the combat.

Preliminary deployment is usually conducted during movement.

123. The order to perform a preliminary deployment is usually given by the battalion or regimental commander. If the enemy situation forces to a rapid preliminary deployment, e.g. in case of a sudden encounter with the enemy, it is ordered by the company commander.

c) Attack.

124. The **strength of the** medium company's **attack** lies in its **employment of the whole unit**[115].

Generally certain preconditions facilitate this:

    clarity of terrain,

    elevated firing positions,

    attack width does not exceed 1200 meters.

---

[113] "Entwicklung" literally translated is "development". Yet, we translated it with "full deployment" according to Condell and Zabecki. For further information see the Section "A Note on the Use of 'Deployment' [...]" in Supplement 2.

[114] The literal translation of the German word "Feindwirkung", is "enemy effect".

[115] See Glossary: Employment of the Whole Unit (Einsatz, geschlossen).

125. Die Kompanie gliedert sich zum Angriff in der Regel zum Breitkeil.

Innerhalb der Abteilung kämpft sie meist in zweiter Linie, um das Vorgehen der leichten Kompanien [zu] überwachen und ihnen Feuerschutz geben zu können.

126. Der **Befehl für den Angriff** muß enthalten:

    Feindnachrichten, eigene Lage,

    Nachbarn,

    Absicht der Abteilung (des Regiments),

    Angriffsziel,

    Gliederung der Abteilung,

        der Kompanie,

    Auftrag für die Kompanie,

        für die einzelnen Züge,

    Zusammenwirken mit anderen Waffen,

        Anschluß[116],

        Trennungslinie oder Mittellinie,

    Gelände, Hindernisse,

    Aufträge an Gefechtstroß und Radfahrzeuge,

        I-Gruppe und S-Trupp[117],

    Nachrichtenverbindungen, Stoßlinie [1]),

    Platz des Führers.

127. In stetem Wechsel zwischen Feuer und Bewegung dringt die Kompanie in den Gegner ein und vernichtet ihn.

1)) Siehe Anlage 6.

---

[116] Bzgl. Anschluß siehe Glossar.

[117] Instandsetzungsgruppe und Sanitätstrupp.

125. For the attack the company is usually organized in the inverted wedge.

Within the battalion, it usually fights in the second line, in order to supervise the actions of the light companies and to support them with covering fire.

126. The **attack order** must contain:

    enemy news, own situation,

    neighboring units,

    intention of the battalion (of the regiment),

    objective,

    composition of the battalion,

        of the company,

    mission for the company,

        for the individual platoons,

    coordination with other weapons,

        contact[118],

        boundary line or center line,

    terrain, obstacles,

    assignments for combat trains and wheeled vehicles,

        maintenance section and medical team,

    signal communication, thrust line [1]),

    position of the commander.

127. In constant alternation between fire and movement, the company penetrates the enemy and destroys him.

---

[1]) See Appendix 6.

---

[118] From German "Anschluß", which in this case is translated with "contact". It refers to a person, vehicle or unit which was used as a reference point. For further information see the Glossary.

128. Der Kompanieführer muß bestrebt sein, die Waffen möglichst vieler Kampfwagen schnell zu **einheitlicher Wirkung** zu bringen.

129. Ist die Kompanie im **I. Treffen** eingesetzt, hat sie meist die Aufgabe, zunächst die feindlichen Panzerabwehrwaffen, dann die Artillerie zu vernichten.

Sie durchstößt hierzu, ohne sich aufhalten zu lassen, schnell die gesamte feindliche Widerstandszone und kämpft dabei erkannte schwere Waffen und Widerstandsnester nieder, soweit sie nicht durch Kampf gegen feindliche Panzerabwehrwaffen gebunden ist. Teile der Kompanie müssen stets bereit sein, Panzerabwehrwaffen sofort unter wirksames Feuer zu nehmen.

130. Die **Aufgabe** der mittleren Kompanie im **II. Treffen** ist die Niederkämpfung aller besonders starken Widerstandsnester in der Tiefenzone.

131. Sie fährt meist am Anfang des II. Treffens, um das I. Treffen schnell und wirksam unterstützen zu können, falls es auf starken Feindwiderstand stößt.

132. Der Kompanieführer kann für den Angriff seiner Kompanie Richtung, Anschluß und Sprünge befehlen. Er teilt nach dem Gelände die Abschnitte für Beobachtung und Feuerüberwachung ein.

128. The company commander must strive to rapidly employ the weapons of as many combat vehicles as possible to a **coordinated effect**[119].

129. When the company is committed in the **I. wave** it usually has the task to destroy the enemy anti-tank weapons first, and then the artillery.

Without being stopped, it quickly penetrates the entire enemy resistance zone and fights down detected heavy weapons and pockets of resistance, as long as it is not bound by enemy anti-tank weapons. Parts of the company must always be ready to immediately take anti-tank weapons under effective fire.

130. The **task** of the medium company in the **II. wave** is to put out of action particularly strong resistance nests in the zone of resistance[120].

131. It usually drives at the front of the II. wave in order to be able to support the I. wave quickly and effectively if it encounters strong enemy resistance.

132. The company commander can order, for his company, attack direction, contact[121] and bounds. In reference to the terrain, he assigns[122] sectors for observation and overwatch.

---

[119] The literal translation of the German "einheitlicher Wirkung" would be "unified effect".

[120] The literal translation of the German word "Tiefenzone" is "Depth zone". This identifies an area, often staggered in depth, that provides resistance to the advance of the tank units.

[121] From German "Anschluß", which in this case is translated with "contact". It refers to a person, vehicle or unit which was used as a reference point. For further information see the Glossary.

[122] From the German word "einteilen / teilt ein". The root verb "teilen" means divide or share, whereas "einteilen" means assign, arrange, etc.

Die Sprünge dürfen nur so groß sein, wie Gelände und der durch die eingeteilten Züge sicherzustellende Feuerschutz es zulassen.

133. Durch rechtzeitiges und schnelles Nachziehen der zum Feuerschutz eingeteilten Züge und Halbzüge wird das flüssige Vorgehen der Kompanie gewährleistet.

Angriff aus der Bewegung.

134. Rasches Handeln des Kompanieführers, Schnelligkeit der Bewegungen und stete Feuerbereitschaft der Waffen befähigen die mittlere Panzerkompanie auch dann aus der Bewegung heraus anzugreifen, wenn der Feind einen Vorsprung in der Gefechtsbereitschaft hat.

135. Greift die Kompanie aus der Bewegung heraus an, ist meist ein kurzer Aufmarschhalt erforderlich, um die Kampfgliederung herzustellen. Er soll möglichst gedeckt gegen feindlichen Sicht- und Waffenwirkung sein.

136. Oft wird es Aufgabe der Kompanie sein, bei überraschendem Zusammenstoß mit dem Feinde den leichten Kompanien beim Einnehmen der Kampfgliederung den Feuerschutz zu geben.

137. Der **Angriffsbefehl** wird oft nur durch Funk in kurzer Form gegeben werden können.

The bounds may only be as far as the terrain and the for covering fire assigned platoons allow.

133. The timely and rapid follow-up of the platoons and half-platoons assigned for covering fire ensures the smooth advance of the company.

Attack from March Column[123].

134. Rapid action by the company commander, speed of movements and constant fire readiness enable the medium tank company to attack from the movement even if the enemy has a head start in his readiness for action.

135. If the company attacks from the move, a short assembly stop is usually required to move into combat formation[124]. It should be as covered as possible against enemy detection and weapons[125].

136. It will often be the company's task, in the event of a surprising clash with the enemy, to give fire support to the light companies while it establishes its tactical grouping.

137. It is often only possible to give the **attack order** by radio in short form.

---

[123] "Angriff aus der Bewegung" literally means "attack from the movement". The equivalent in the US Field Manual FM 17-32: The Tank Company, light and medium from 1942 is "attack from march column".

[124] From the German "Kampfgliederung", which could also be translated into "tactical grouping".

[125] "Sicht- und Waffeneffekt" literally means "sight- and weapon effect".

Er muß mindestens enthalten:
- Feind,
- Angriffsziel,
- Gliederung,
- Anschluß[126].

138. Beim Angriff aus der Bewegung kommt es besonders darauf an, alle Waffen schnell zur Wirkung zu bringen. Dies wird erreicht

durch Bilden des „Breitkeils", wobei der rückwärtige Zug aus überhöhender Stellung schießt, oder

durch Herstellen der „Geöffneten Linie" (Einschieben des rückwärtigen Zuges in die Feuerfront).

Angriff aus der Bereitstellung.

139. Treffen Panzerkräfte auf abwehrbereiten Gegner, stellen sie sich in der Regel zum Angriff bereit.

Die Kompanie gliedert sich in der Bereitstellung zum Angriff, soweit Raum und Gelände es zulassen.

140. Die Erkundung des Bereitstellungsraumes erfolgt in der Regel durch den Erkunderzug der Abteilung. Durch diesen wird die Kompanie in ihren Bereitstellungsraum geführt.

---

[126] Bzgl. Anschluß siehe Glossar.

It must contain at least:

> enemy,
>
> objective,
>
> composition,
>
> contact[127].

138. When attacking from movement, it is particularly important to quickly bring all weapons to bear. This will be achieved

> by forming the "inverted wedge" with the rear platoon firing from an elevated position, or
>
> by creating the "open line" (shifting the rear platoon to the fire front).

Attack from Assembly Areas.

139. When tank forces meet an enemy ready to defend, they usually prepare attack formations[128].

The company arranges itself in the assembly area for the attack as far as space and terrain allow.

140. As a rule, reconnaissance of the assembly area[129] is carried out by the recon platoon of the battalion. This [recon platoon] leads the company into its assembly area.

---

[127] From the German "Anschluß", which in this case is translated with "contact". It refers to a person, vehicle or unit which was used as a reference point. For further information see the Glossary.

[128] As you can see, Captain Obvious also served in the Wehrmacht.

[129] Nowadays usually referred to as the TAA, Tactical Assembly Area.

141. In der Bereitstellung werden die letzten Vorbereitungen für den Angriff getroffen. Dazu sind vorausschauend die hierfür notwendigen Teile des Trosses heranzuziehen.

142. Das Einfahren in die Bereitstellung muß lautlos geschehen (niedrige Motorendrehzahl). Tarnung gegen Erd- und Luftbeobachtung ist besonders wichtig.

Erdaufwürfe, die durch Lenkbewegungen entstanden sind, müssen beseitigt werden, um der feindlichen Luftaufklärung das Vorhandensein von Panzerkampfwagen zu verbergen.

143. Der Kompanieführer muß befehlen:

    Zeit der Gefechtsbereitschaft,

    Art der Sicherung,

    Verbleib des Trosses,

    Platz des Kompanieführers.

144. Die **Sicherung** der Kompanie in der Bereitstellung übernimmt der leichte Zug, wenn sie nicht durch die leichten Kompanien oder durch andere Truppen erfolgt.

145. Die **Fliegerabwehr** regelt die Abteilung. Kämpft die Kompanie allein, hat sie Luftspähposten auszustellen [sic!][130], die gleichzeitig Fliegerwarnung geben. Wenn die Lage es erlaubt, sind einzelne M. G. aus den Wagen auszubauen und zur Fliegerabwehr einzusetzen.

---

[130] Möglicherweise sollte dies wohl „aufzustellen" heißen.

141. In the assembly area, the final preparations for the attack are made. For this purpose, the necessary parts of the trains must be gathered.

142. The entry into the assembly area must be done silently (low engine speed). Camouflage against ground and air observation is particularly important.

Track marks and skids[131] caused by steering movements must be removed in order to conceal the presence of tanks from enemy aerial reconnaissance.

143. The company commander must give the order:

> time of combat readiness,
>
> type of security,
>
> whereabouts of the train,
>
> position of the company commander.

144. The light platoon assumes responsibility for **securing** the company in the assembly area if it is not carried out by the light company or by other troops.

145. The **anti-aircraft defense** is controlled by the battalion. If the company fights alone, it has to setup[132] anti-aircraft lookouts, which also provide air raid warnings. If the situation permits, individual M. G.s must be removed from the vehicles and used for anti-aircraft defense.

---

[131] From the German word "Erdaufwürfe", literally translating to "Earth throw ups". Meant are ground marks caused by tracks that could led enemy forces in identifying the presence of a friendly tank unit.

[132] In the original there was "auszustellen" (to issue) which very likely should have been "aufzustellen" (to setup).

146. Die Zugführer sind, wenn Zeit und Gelände es gestatten, durch Einblick in das voraussichtliche Angriffsgelände vom Kompanieführer einzuweisen. Gestattet die Feindlage oder das Gelände dies nicht, müssen Karte und Luftbilder zur Einweisung in Lage und Angriffsplan benutzt werden.

147. Das Einhalten der Funkstille ist besonders zu beachten, um dem Feind nicht vorzeitig die Anwesenheit von Panzern zu verraten.

d) Kampf unter besonderen Verhältnissen.

Kampf im Nebel und bei Dunkelheit.

148. Der Angriff im Nebel und bei Dunkelheit kann besonders dann notwendig werden, wenn es gilt, einen bereits erschütterten Gegner zu vernichten und zu völliger Auflösung zu bringen.

149. Innerhalb der Kompanie sind die Abstände und Zwischenräume so weit zu verringern, daß die Sichtverbindung zwischen den Panzerkampfwagen aufrechterhalten bleibt. Die Richtung ist mit dem Kreiselkompaß zu halten.

Das Einhalten der Richtung wird erleichtert, wenn Wege und deutlich erkennbare Geländeabschnitte in Richtung auf das Ziel führen.

150. Im Nebel, in der Dämmerung und bei Dunkelheit kann die Kompanie den Angriff nur von Abschnitt zu Abschnitt führen, um den Zusammenhang der Kräfte immer wieder sicherzustellen.

146. When time and terrain permit, platoon leaders are briefed by the company commander by surveying the anticipated attack area. If enemy position or the terrain does not permit this, maps and aerial photographs must be used to advise [the unit] on the position and plan of attack.

147. Special attention shall be paid to maintaining radio silence so as not to prematurely reveal the presence of tanks to the enemy.

d) Combat under Special Circumstances.

Combat in Fog and Darkness.

148. The attack during fog and darkness can become particularly necessary, if it is required to destroy an already shaken enemy and to bring him to complete dissolution.

149. Within the company, the distances and spaces are reduced so as to maintain line of sight between the tanks. The direction is to be held with the course gyro.

Keeping the direction is made easier if paths and clearly visible terrain sections lead towards the objective.

150. In fog, twilight and darkness, the company can only conduct the attack from section to section to ensure the cohesion of forces.

Leuchtpatronen, Leuchtfallschirme der Flieger oder in Brand geschossene Strohmieten und Häuser erleichtern dem Panzerkampfwagen das Auffinden der Ziele.

151. Beim Durchfahren von künstlichem Nebel ist zu beachten, daß die Panzerkampfwagen dem Feind nach Durchstoßen der Nebelwand oder -Zone ein besonders gutes Ziel bieten.

Nach Durchstoßen des Nebels ist daher die Geschwindigkeit schnell zu erhöhen und die Zwischenräume sind wieder zu vergrößern.

Das gleiche gilt beim Aufreißen des natürlichen Nebels.

152. Der leichte Zug fährt, wenn er nicht mit der Gefechtsaufklärung oder mit Flankenschutz beauftragt ist, so vor der Kompanie, daß er sie vor einem plötzlichen Aufprallen auf den Gegner, besonders auf Pak und Minen frühzeitig warnen kann.

153. Häufig werden Panzerangriffe im Morgengrauen geführt, um mit dem ersten „Büchsenlicht" in den Feind einzubrechen. Eingehende Gelände- und Wegeerkundung schon während der Nacht und Bezeichnung der Anmarschwege sind Voraussetzungen für den Einsatz der Kompanie.

Signal cartridges, illuminating aerial parachutes or straw stacks and houses set ablaze by weapon's fire[133] make it easier for the tank to find the targets.

151. When driving through artificial smoke, it should be noted that the tank offers the enemy a particularly good target after penetrating the smoke wall or zone.

Therefore, after piercing the fog, the speed must be increased quickly, and the spacing is extended again.

The same applies when natural fog[134] dissipates.

152. The light platoon, if it is not in charge of combat reconnaissance or flank protection, travels in front of the company in such a manner that it can issue a timely warning of a sudden appearance of enemy forces, anti-tank guns and mines.

153. Frequently, tank-attacks are led in the dawn in order to break into the enemy with the first "hunting-light[135]". Detailed reconnaissance of terrain and track already conducted during the previous night and the designation of the approach routes are prerequisites for the employment of the company.

---

[133] Specifically set ablaze by use of weaponry. The manual does not specific whether cannon fire, flare guns, or other arms are to be used but the German phrasing "in Brand geschossene" (lit. translation: set ablaze by [gun] fire) could indicate the use of the tank's armament.

[134] In German "smoke" is called "artificial fog", thus the term "natural fog".

[135] From the German word "Büchsenlicht", literally translating to "rifle light". This is a term originating from hunting terminology, indicating the specific light spectrum seen during dawn and dusk. Sometimes referred to as "golden hour" in photography.

Angriff über Flüsse.

154. Beim Kampf um Flußübergänge wird es vornehmlich Aufgabe der mittleren Kompanie sein, den Feuerschutz für das Übersetzen und den Angriff über den Fluß für die leichten Kompanien oder die Schützen zu übernehmen.

155. Die einzelnen Züge müssen am diesseitigen Ufer so in halb verdeckte Feuerstellungen gehen, daß sie feindliche Widerstandnester schnell unter zusammengefaßtes Feuer nehmen können.

Rascher Wechsel der Feuerstellungen ist meist geboten, damit der Gegner auf dem jenseitigen Ufer keine Zeit zur wirksamen Bekämpfung des einzelnen Panzerkampfwagens gewinnt.

Kampf im Wald und im Gebirge.

156. Der geschlossene Einsatz der Kompanie bildet die Ausnahme. In der Regel werden Halbzüge oder einzelne Wagen die angreifenden Schützen beim Vorgehen unterstützen.

157. Beim Kampf im Wald ist die Gefahr plötzlicher Überfälle durch den Feind aus nächster Entfernung besonders groß. Durch verschärfte Aufmerksamkeit muß der Feuerschutz der Panzerkampfwagen untereinander gewährleistet werden (siehe Ziffer 72).

Attack across Rivers.

154. During combat at river crossings, the primary task of the medium company is to provide protective fire for the crossing and attack of the light companies or riflemen.

155. The individual platoons must move into semi-concealed firing positions on the already controlled riverbank so that they can quickly open concentrated fire on enemy pockets of resistance on the opposing riverbank.

A fast alteration of the firing positions is usually required so that the enemy on the other riverbank does not have the time to conduct effective fire against individual tanks.

Combat in Forests and Mountains.

156. Employment of the whole unit[136] as a company is the exception. As a rule, half-platoons or individual vehicles will support the attacking riflemen.

157. When fighting in the forest, the danger of sudden attacks by the enemy from close distance is particularly heightened. Increased attention must be paid to provide constant covering fire among the tanks (see Number 72).

---

[136] See Glossary: Employment of the Whole Unit (Einsatz, geschlossen).

158. Im Gebirge ist der Einsatz vorher besonders sorgfältig zu erkunden, da der Panzerkampfwagen meist an die Straße gebunden ist.

Zum Überwinden stark eingeschnittener Abschnitte wird die Kompanie häufig zum Feuerschutz eingesetzt werden. Er wird nach den Grundsätzen der Ziffer 155 gegeben.

V. Angriff gegen eine durch ständige Anlagen verstärkte Stellung.

159. Beim Angriff gegen befestigte Stellungen ist engste Zusammenarbeit zwischen der Kompanie mit der zu Fuß angreifenden Truppe erforderlich.

Wieviel Kräfte für die Aufgaben einzusetzen sind und welche Aufgaben diese zu erfüllen haben, befiehlt der Führer, dem die Kompanie unterstellt ist.

Meist wird es Aufgabe der Kompanie sein, mit Teilen Feuerschutz für das Vorarbeiten der angreifenden Stoßtrupps zu geben, mit Teilen aus nahen Entfernungen durch Beschuß der Scharten den Feind in den ständigen Anlagen niederzuringen.

160. In der Regel werden den Führern der Stoßtrupps der zu Fuß angreifenden Truppe nur einzelne Halbzüge, in Ausnahmefällen Züge oder die ganze Kompanie unterstellt. Die übrigen Teile der Kompanie befinden sich dann bei der Panzerabteilung, die erst nach Schaffen von Gassen zum Angriff antritt.

158. In the mountains, an operation must be examined carefully in advance, since the tank is usually tied to the road.

The company will often be used for fire support to overcome bottled necked sections. It shall be given in accordance with the principles set out in Number 155.

V. Attack against a Position Reinforced by Permanent Installations.

159. When attacking fortified positions, close cooperation is required between the company and the troops attacking by foot.

The commander, to whom the company is subordinated, will outline how many forces are to be used and which tasks these have to fulfill.

Usually it will be the company's task to provide covering fire during the preparatory work of the attacking assault detachments on the one hand, and, from close distances, wear down the enemy in the permanent installations by firing at the embrasures.

160. As a rule, the commanders of the assault detachments will be provided with individual half-platoons and only in exceptional cases, platoons, or the whole company. The remaining parts of the company remain with the armored group, which only starts to attack after attack routes have been established.

161. Im Hinblick darauf, daß die wirksame Schußentfernung der Panzerkampfwagen gering und nur direktes Richten möglich ist, ist ein Festlegen der einzelnen Feuerstellungen vorher anzustreben. Dem Panzerführer muß Gelegenheit gegeben werden, bei Tageslicht die Stellung selbst zu erkunden.

Die Erkundung muß sich auch auf Anmarschwege und Wechselstellungen erstrecken.

162. Um die Überraschung zu wahren, ist es zweckmäßig, die Panzerkampfwagen im Laufe der Nacht auf 5 bis 7 km heranzuführen und erst unmittelbar vor Angriffsbeginn in die vorderste Linie der Sicherung bzw. in die erste Feuerstellung vorzuziehen.

163. Die erste Stellung wird oft in der Linie liegen, aus der die Schützen zum Angriff antreten. Oft werden die Panzerkampfwagen aber auch aus dieser Linie mit den Schützen zusammen einen oder mehrere Sprünge vorwärts machen müssen, ehe sie ihre erste Feuerstellung einnehmen. Je dichter die Panzerkampfwagen an die Infanterie herangehalten werden, desto sicherer ist die Zusammenarbeit.

Wirkung geht vor Deckung!

164. Die Panzerkampfwagen IV können den Angriff der Schützen aus rückwärtigen Stellungen

161. Considering that the effective firing range of the tanks is short and only direct fire is possible, individual firing positions should be specified beforehand. The tank commander must be given the opportunity to explore the position himself in daylight.

Such reconnaissance must also cover approach routes and alternative positions.

162. To preserve the element of surprise, it is advisable to close the tanks to about 5 to 7 km of the target throughout the night and to advance them only immediately before the start of the attack to either the foremost security line or to the first firing position.

163. The first position will often be along the line from which the riflemen will attack. Often the tanks will have to make one or more bounds forward from this line together with the riflemen, before they take their first firing positions. The closer the tanks are kept to the infantry, the more assured the cooperation is.

Effect takes precedence over cover!

164. The Panzerkampfwagen IV can monitor the attack of the riflemen from rear positions

nur im ersten Teil des Angriffes überwachen, solange die Schützen noch in Reihe vorgehen und genügend breite Lücken vorhanden sind. Ein Überschießen ist bei der Kürze der Entfernung nur bei besonders günstigem Gelände möglich.

Sobald die Schützen gezwungen sind, sich zu entwickeln, gehören die Panzerkampfwagen in ihre unmittelbare Nähe. Durch sorgfältige Einzelerkundung muß vermieden werden, daß Panzerkampfwagen Stellungen wählen, die im flankierenden Feuer panzerbrechender Waffen liegen.

165. Die Panzerkampfwagen dürfen sich nicht scheuen, näher an die feindliche Stellung heranzufahren und – wenn nicht anders möglich – auch ohne jede Deckung in Stellung zu gehen, um jeden sichtbaren Feind durch Feuer zu vernichten.

166. Am Einbruch in das feindliche Hindernis nehmen die Panzerkampfwagen nicht teil, weil sie dazu nicht befähigt sind. Sie bleiben in ihrer letzten Stellung dicht vor den feindlichen Hindernissen stehen und überwachen aus nächster Entfernung die Arbeit der Stroßtrupps zum Öffnen von Gassen.

167. Die Panzerkampfwagen beteiligen sich nach dem Einbruch an der Vernichtung des Feindes zwischen den Befestigungsanlagen und nisten sich zum Halten der gewonnenen Stellung ein. Ein sofortiger Durchbruch dieser Panzerkampfwagen in

only during the first part of the attack, provided the riflemen advance in line and there are enough wide gaps. Overhead fire is only possible when the distance remains short and the terrain is particularly favorable.

As soon as the riflemen are forced to perform a full deployment[137], the tanks belong in their immediate vicinity. By careful individual reconnaissance it must be avoided that tanks choose positions which makes them subject to flanking fire of armor-piercing weapons.

165. The tanks should not shy away from moving closer to the enemy position and - if not otherwise possible - to take up position without any cover in order to destroy any visible enemy by fire.

166. The tanks do not take part in the break-in of the enemy obstacle because they are not qualified to do so. They remain in their last position close to the enemy obstacles and, from a close distance, monitor the work of the assault detachment opening approach lanes.

167. After the break-in, the tanks take part in the destruction of the enemy in the midst of the fortification network and prepare[138] to hold the gained position. An immediate penetration of these tanks in

---

[137] See Supplement 2, Section "A Note on the Use of 'Deployment' [...]" for further information.

[138] The literal translation of the German "nisten sich" would be "to nest" / "settle down".

die Tiefe wird nur in Ausnahmefällen möglich sein (starker Munitionsverbrauch).

In gleicher Weise wird der Angriff gegen weitere, rückwärtige Stellungen fortgeführt, wozu meist ein neuer Befehl des Schützenführers und Munitionsergänzung erforderlich sind.

168. Sobald die feindliche Stellung, die aus mehreren Widerstandslinien bestehen kann, in planmäßigem Angriff durchbrochen ist, werden zurückgehaltene Teile des Panzerverbandes zum Stoß in die Tiefe angesetzt.

169. Aufgabe der mittleren Kompanie kann es sein, im Rahmen des Panzerverbandes schnell bis an den rückwärtigen Rand der Stellung durchzustoßen, wenn der Einbruch in die feindliche Stellung gelungen ist. Gegenangriffe des Feindes können so am wirksamsten zerschlagen werden.

VI. Kampf „Panzer gegen Panzer".

170. Die mittlere Panzerkompanie ist auf Grund der Bestückung ihrer Panzerkampfwagen mit 7,5 cm Kw. K. und deren Ausstattung mit Panzergranaten besonders geeignet, feindliche Panzerkampfwagen zu vernichten.

Der **geschlossene Einsatz** der Kompanie ist die Regel.

depth will only be possible in exceptional cases (heavy ammunition consumption).

The attack against further rear positions is continued in similar fashion, although this usually requires a new order from the infantry commander[139] and replenishment of ammunition.

168. As soon as the enemy position, which may consist of several defensive lines, is overcome, retained elements of the tank formation are to thrust into depth.

169. If the penetration of the enemy position was successful, it can be the task of the medium company, as part of the armored group, to quickly break-in to the hindmost section of the defensive positions. This is the most effective way to smash enemy counterattacks.

VI. Combat "Tanks vs. Tanks".

170. As the medium tank company's tanks are equipped with the 7.5 cm Kw. K. and armor-piercing shells, they are particularly suited to the destruction of enemy tanks.

The **employment of the whole unit**[140] of the company is the rule.

---

[139] The German "Schützenführer" literally translates to "riflemen leader".

[140] See Glossary: Employment of the Whole Unit (Einsatz, geschlossen).

171. Rasches Handeln und schlagartige Eröffnung des Feuers aller verfügbaren panzerbrechenden Waffen auf wirkungsvolle Entfernung, möglichst aus verdeckter Stellung und aus unerwarteter Richtung sind die Mittel, um die Überlegenheit sicherzustellen.

172. Stößt die Kompanie unvermutet auf feindliche Panzerkampfwagen, so muß der Kompanieführer durch Schießen mit Nebelgranaten der Kompanie bzw. der Abteilung das Bilden einer Feuerfront ermöglichen.

173. Sämtliche Panzerkampfwagen der mittleren Kompanie müssen schnell zur vollen Wirkung kommen. Der Kompanieführer muß seine Kompanie fest in der Hand behalten. Kein Zug darf sich im Eifer des Gefechts selbstständig machen.

174. Ob die Kompanie gegen Flanke oder Rücken der feindlichen Panzerkampfwagen eingesetzt wird, befiehlt der Führer des Panzerverbandes (Abteilungs- oder Regimentsführer).

175. Weicht der Gegner, so stößt die Kompanie unverzüglich nach, um ihn zu verfolgen und zu vernichten.

VII. Verhalten beim Auftreffen auf Minen.

176. Minen werden oft nur dadurch erkannt werden können, daß die vordersten Panzerkampfwagen auf Minen aufgefahren sind. Es kommt in

171. Rapid action and immediate opening of fire from all available armor-piercing weapons at effective range, preferably from a concealed position and from an unexpected direction, are the means to ensure superiority.

172. If the company unexpectedly encounters enemy tanks, the company commander must enable the company or battalion to form a firing line by using smoke shells.

173. All tanks of the medium company need to be readily employed to full effect. The company commander must keep his company under firm control. Throughout the engagement, no platoon must become independent.

174. The commander of the tank formation (battalion or regimental commander) will decide whether the company is to be used against the flanks or rear of the enemy tanks.

175. If the enemy evades, the company pushes immediately after [him], in order to pursue and destroy.

VII. Actions upon Encountering a Minefield.

176. Mines will often only be detected by the fact that the foremost tanks have hit[141] mines. In this case

---

[141] The literal translation of the German word "auf Minen aufgefahren", is "having driven on mines".

diesem Falle darauf an, zu verhindern, daß weitere Panzerkampfwagen den Minen zum Opfer fallen.

177. Zu diesem Zweck hat jeder mit Sender ausgestattete Führerpanzerkampfwagen beim Bemerken der Zerstörung eines eigenen Panzerkampfwagens durch Minen den Funkspruch zu geben:

„**Xte Kompanie!** (Deckname) – **Minen! – Halt! – Minen! – Halt! – Minen! – Halt!**"
„**Ein Panzerkampfwagen Xter Zug** (Deckname) **bei Busch halb rechts (Beispiel) auf Mine gelaufen!**"

178. Auf den Spruch „**Minen! – Halt!**" stellt die Kompanie die Vorwärtsbewegung ein.

Die vordersten Kampfwagen, die vielleicht schon in das Minenfeld eingedrungen sind, setzen in ihrer Spur zurück. Der Kompanieführer meldet der Abteilung und erhält von dieser weitere Befehle für rückwärtiges Sammeln oder Ansatz in einer anderen Richtung.

179. Kommt beim Auftreffen auf Minen gleichzeitig feindliche Panzerabwehr zur Wirkung, blenden die Panzerkampfwagen IV bei günstigen Windverhältnissen den Feind durch Beschuß mit Nebel. Der Feuerschutz für die leichten Kompanien ist auch ohne Befehl zu geben.

it is important, to prevent further tanks from falling victim to the mines.

177. For this purpose, every commander tank equipped with a transmitter shall give a radio message following the destruction of its own tanks by mines:

"**X Company!** (cover name) **Mines! - Stop! - Mines! - Stop! - Mines! - Stop!** "**A tank X Zug** (cover name) **at a bush half right** (example) **hit a mine!**"

178. Upon receiving the message[142] "**Mines! - Stop!**" the company stops moving forward.

The foremost tanks, which may already have entered the minefield, retrace their steps along their tracks. The company commander reports to the battalion and receives further orders from the battalion for rearward assembly or to approach from a different direction.

179. If mines are hit while simultaneously facing enemy anti-tank defenses, Panzerkampfwagen IVs will fire smoke rounds at the defenses if favorable wind conditions allow them to thereby blind the enemy. Covering fire for the light companies is to be given without orders.

---

[142] The literal translation of the German "Auf den Spruch" would be "On the phrase".

VIII. Zusammenwirken mit der Stabskompanie.

180. Bei Märschen, Rasten und beim Einnehmen von Bereitstellungen wird die Kompanie durch den **Erkunderzug** der Stabskompanie eingewiesen.

181. Zur **Fliegerabwehr** können Teile des Fliegerabwehrzuges der Stabskompanie in die Kompanie beim Marsch und in der Bereitstellung eingegliedert werden.

Die bei der Kompanie für den Luftschutz eingesetzten Teile wirken mit diesem Trupp zusammen.

182. Der **Pionierzug** wird zum Beseitigen und Überwinden von Hindernissen auf dem Marsch, beim entfalteten Vorgehen, in der Bereitstellung und vor dem Angriff durch die Abteilung eingesetzt. Teile können für Sonderaufträge der Kompanie unmittelbar unterstellt werden.

Sicherung der Pionierarbeiten in Feindnähe durch eingesetzte Überwachungswagen muß von der Kompanie gewährleistet sein.

IX. Instandsetzung und Versorgung.

183. Für den Einsatz der Kfz.-Instandsetzungsgruppe gelten die Bestimmungen der „Vorläufigen Anweisung für den Einsatz der Kfz.-Instandsetzungsgruppen der Panzereinheiten und für die Ausbildung von Panzerwarten und Panzerfunkwarten" vom 26. März 1941.

VIII. Coordinating with Headquarters Company.

180. During marches, rests, and moving into assembly areas, the company is instructed by the **recon platoon** of the headquarters company.

181. For **anti-aircraft defense,** parts of the anti-aircraft platoon of the headquarters company may be integrated into the company during the march and in the assembly area.

The elements of the company assigned to air defense cooperate with this unit.

182. The **engineer platoon** is used to remove and overcome obstacles during the march, during advancing after the preliminary deployment[143], in the assembly area and before the attack by the battalion. Elements can be directly subordinated to the company for special orders.

The company must overwatch the activities of the engineers in close proximity to the enemy.

IX. Maintenance and Supply.

183. For the assignment of the vehicle maintenance section the regulation "Provisional Instructions for the Operation of the Vehicle Maintenance Sections of the Tank Units and for the Training of Tank Maintenance Crews and Tank Radio Maintenance Crews" of 26 March 1941 applies.

---

[143] Since we translated "Entfaltung" with "preliminary deployment" the translation of "entfalteten" is a bit a cumbersome, since in this instance it is not used as a noun. For further information see the Section "A Note on the Use of 'Deployment' [...]" in Supplement 2.

184. Ausschlaggebend für die ständige Gefechtsbereitschaft ist die planmäßige Versorgung der Kompanie vor allem mit Betriebsstoff und Munition. Der Kompanieführer muß stets die Versorgung seiner Kompanie überwachen. Alle Unterführer, besonders der Schirrmeister[144] und der Hauptfeldwebel, müssen ihn bei dieser Aufgabe unterstützen.

185. Die Ergänzung von Munition, Betriebsstoff und Verpflegung erfolgt bei den Versorgungseinrichtungen der Division und wird durch diese befohlen. Die Versorgung ist nur gewährleistet, wenn die Meldungen über den Bedarf schnell zur Abteilung gelangen.

---

[144] Er war der Kraftfahrzeug-Meister des Fuhrparks der Einheit und damit der Hauptverantwortliche für die Kraftfahrzeuge. Der Name geht auf die militärische Nutzung von Pferden zurück („Pferdegeschirr".) die aber auch noch von der Wehrmacht in einer großen Stückzahl eingesetzt wurden.

184. Punctual delivery of supplies, primarily of fuel and ammunition, is the decisive factor in ensuring a permanent combat readiness of the company. The company commander must always supervise the inventory of his company. All subordinate commanders, especially the maintenance technical sergeant[145] and the company sergeant major, must support him in this task.

185. The provisioning of ammunition, fuel and rations takes place at the division's supply depots and is supervised by them. A resupply is only guaranteed if reports outlining the demand reach the battalion quickly.

---

[145] The literal translation of the German word "Schirrmeister" is "Horse tackle master". This is a composite word from "Pferdegeschirr", a horse harness or tackle and "Meister", master. As the maintenance technical sergeant, the "Schirrmeister" was responsible for the vehicles of the unit.

Erläuterungen der im Text angewandten Zeichen.

Anlage 1

- ⌸ Gruppenführer-Panzerkampfwagen.
- ⌸ Halbzugführer-Panzerkampfwagen.
- ⌸ Zugführer-Panzerkampfwagen.
- ⌸ Kompanieführer-Panzerkampfwagen.
- ⊠ Panzerkampfwagen II.
- ⊠ Panzerkampfwagen III.
- ⊠ Panzerkampfwagen IV.
- ⦵ Kompanieführer.
- ⦵ Zugführer.   [Verwendete/Fehlende Darstellungen]
- ⦵ Halbzugführer.   ● Gruppenführer.
- ⦵ Panzerführer.   [So angegeben, aber im Text nicht verwendet.]   ● Panzerführer.
- ⦵ Richtschütze.
- Ö Ladeschütze.
- △ Panzerfahrer.
- ⓢ Panzerfunker.
- ○ Panzerschütze.

Explanations of the symbols used in the text.

Appendix 1

- ⊟ Section leader tank.
- ⊟ Half-platoon leader tank.
- ⊟ Platoon leader tank.
- ⊟ Company commander tank.
- ⊠ Panzerkampfwagen II.
- ⊠ Panzerkampfwagen III.
- ⊠ Panzerkampfwagen IV.
- ● Company commander.
- ● Platoon leader.
- ● Half-platoon leader.
- ○ Tank commander.
- ○ Gunner.
- ○ Loader.
- △ Tank driver.
- ⊙ Tank radio operator.
- ○ Tank rifleman.

[Used / Additional Figures]

- ● Section leader.
- ● Tank commander.

[Indicated here, yet not used in the text.]

EN-77

Anlage 2

Stärkenachweisung der mittleren Panzerkompanie an Kraftfahrzeugen.

(Anhalt)

a) Gruppe Führer:

    5 Pz. Kpfw. II,

    2 Pz. Kpfw. IV,

        1 m. gl. Pkw. [146] Kfz. 15 (m. Gerätschaften),

        3 m. Kräder[147].

b) 1. bis 3. Zug:

    4 Pz. Kpfw. IV.

c) Staffel für Wechselbesatzung:

    3 l. gl. Lkw.[148] (offen).

d) Gefechtstroß:

    1 m. gl. Pkw. Kfz. 15 (m. Gerätschaften)

    10 m. gl. Lkw., davon

        1 für gr. Feldkochherd,

        4 für Munition,

        1 für Betriebsstoff,

        3 für Betriebst.-Transport,

        1 für Gerät u. Mansch. Transport,

    2 s. Kräder m. Bw.

---

[146] Mittelschwerer geländegängiger Personenkraftwagen.

[147] Mittlere Kräder ist die Kurzform von Krafträder – alte Bezeichnung für Motorrad.

[148] Leichter geländegängiger Lastkraftwagen.

Appendix 2

Table of Organization of Motor Vehicles for the Medium Tank Company.
(Orientation)

a) Commander's section:

    5 Pz. Kpfw. II,

    2 Pz. Kpfw. IV,

        1 medium cross-country capable vehicle Kfz. 15 (with equipment),

        3 medium motorcycles.

b) 1st to 3rd platoon:

    4 Pz. Kpfw. IV.

c) Element for replacement crew:

    3 light cross-country capable trucks (open-topped).

d) Combat train:

    1 medium cross-country capable vehicle Kfz. 15 (with equipment)

    10 medium cross-country capable trucks, of which

        1 for large field kitchen,

        4 for ammunition,

        1 for fuel,

        3 for fuel transport,

        1 for equipment and personnel transport,

    2 heavy motorcycles with sidecar.

e) Kfz.-Instandsetzungsgruppe:
    1 Inst. Kfz. 2/40,
    1 m. gl. Lkw. Für Ers. Teile u. Gerät[149],
    2 l. Zgkw.[150] (1 to) Sd. Kfz. 10,
    3 s. Kräder m. Bw.[151]

f) Gepäck-Troß:
    1 m. Lkw. (3 to) für Gepäck,
    1 m. Krad.

---

[149] Mittelschwerer geländegängiger Lastkraftwagen für Ersatzteile und Gerät.
[150] Leichter Zugkraftwagen.
[151] Schwere Kräder mit Beiwagen.

e) Vehicle maintenance section:
- 1 maintenance vehicle Kfz. 2/40,
- 1 medium cross-country capable truck for spare parts and equipment,
- 2 light half-tracks (1 t[152]) Sd. Kfz. 10,
- 3 heavy motorcycles with sidecar.

f) Baggage train:
- 1 medium truck (3 t) for baggage,
- 1 medium motorcycle.

---

[152] Metric ton; equals 1000 kilograms or 2205 pounds.

Anlage 3

Taktische Zahlenangaben für die mittlere Panzerkompanie.

1. Gefechtsstärke der Kompanie:

14 Pz. Kpf. Wg. IV (7,5 cm),

5 Pz. Kpf. Wg. II (2 cm).

Panzerbewaffnung:

14 Kampfwagenkanonen 7,5 cm,

5 Kampfwagenkanonen 2 cm,

33 Maschinengewehre (M. G. 34).

2. Marschgeschwindigkeit auf guten Straßen und Wegen:

Kampfstaffel: 20 km/std.,

Räderstaffel: 40 km/std.

3. Fahrbereich mit einer Kraftstofffüllung:

Kampfstaffel: 150 km Straße,

                100 km Gelände,

Räderstaffel: 250 km.

4. Betriebsstoffverbrauch auf 100 km:

Vergaserkraftstoff	5 000 l,
Dieselkraftstoff	400 l,
Schmieröl	300 l,
Getriebeöl	30 l,
Fett	30 kg.

Appendix 3

Tactical Figures for the Medium Tank Company.

1. Company combat strength:

14 Pz. Kpf. Wg. IV (7.5 cm),

5 Pz. Kpf. Wg. II (2 cm).

Tank armament:

14 guns 7.5 cm,

5 guns 2 cm,

33 machine guns (M. G. 34).

2. Marching speed on good roads and paths:

combat elements[153]: 20 kph,

wheeled vehicle element: 40 kph.

3. Driving range with one fuel load:

combat echelon: 150 km road,

100 km cross-country,

wheel echelon: 250 km.

4. Fuel consumption per 100 km:

gasoline	5 000 l,
diesel	400 l,
lubricating oil	300 l,
transmission oil	30 l,
grease	30 kg.

---

[153] From the German "Kampfstaffel".

5. Verbrauch der Bremsbeläge in Kettenfahrzeugen:

    in kurvenreichem, bergigem Gelände

        nach etwa   500 km,

        sonst nach etwa 1 000 km.

6. **Straßen unter 3,5 m Breite** sind von der Kampfstaffel nur im Einbahn- oder Blockverkehr benutzbar.

7. **Kampfentfernungen (Schußweiten):**

7,5 cm Kw. K.	2 000 m,
2 cm Kw. K.	800 m,
Turm-M. G.	800 m,
Bug-M. G.	400 m.

8. Munition (Anhalt):

        a) bei der Kampfstaffel:

für **Pz. Kpfw. IV**:

    728 Sprenggranatpatronen (14 x 52),

    280 Panzergranatpatronen (14 x 20),

    112 Nebelgranatpatronen (14 x 8),

je M. G. 1 350 SmK[154]-Patronen, davon die Hälfte mit Leuchtspur.

Für **Pz. Kpfw. II**:

    450 Sprenggranatpatronen (5 x 90),

    450 Panzergranatpatronen (5 x 90),

je M. G. 1 425 SmK-Patronen, davon die Hälfte Leuchtspur.

---

[154] SmK bedeutet Spitzgeschoß mit Kern, d.h. ein Teil des Geschoßes enthielt einen gehärteten Stahlkern.

5. **Usage of brake linings in tracked vehicles:**

    in winding, mountainous terrain

        after about   500 km,

        or after about 1 000 km.

6. **Roads less than 3.5 m wide** can only be used by the combat element in one-way, or by alternating traffic.

7. **Combat distances (firing distances):**

7.5 cm Kw. K.	2 000 m,
2 cm Kw. K.	800 m,
turret-M. G.	800 m,
bow-M. G.	400 m.

8. Ammunition (Orientation):

        a) with the Combat Echelon:

for **Pz. Kpfw. IV:**

    728 explosive shells (14 x 52),

    280 armor-piercing shells (14 x 20),

    112 smoke shells (14 x 8),

for each M. G. 1 350 pointed bullet with hardened steel core cartridges[155], half of which are tracers.

For **Pz. Kpfw. II:**

    450 explosive shells (5 x 90),

    450 armor-piercing shells (5 x 90),

for each M. G. 1 425 pointed bullet with hardened steel core cartridges, half of which are tracers.

---

[155] This refers to SmK ("Spitzgeschoß mit Kern"), literally translating to "pointed projectile with core". "Pointed projectile" is also called "spitzer" in English. This was a hardened steel core projectile of 7.92x57mm Mauser and the standard armour piercing round available to German units in that calibre. Depending on range, it could be effectively used against light cover, such as fences, hedgerows or even light armor plating.

b) beim Gefechtstroß:

für **Pz. Kpfw. IV:**

1 302 Sprenggranatpatronen (14 x 93),

    490 Panzergranatpatronen (14 x 35),

    168 Nebelgranatpatronen (14 x 12),

je M. G. 1 150 SmK-Patronen, davon die Hälft mit Leuchtspur.

für **Pz. Kpfw. II:**

    300 Sprenggranatpatronen (5 x 60),

    300 Panzergranatpatronen (5 x 60),

je M. G. 1 075 SmK-Patronen, davon die Hälfte mit Leuchtspur.

b) with the Combat Train:

for **Pz. Kpfw. IV:**

1 302 explosive shells (14 x 93),

    490 armor-piercing shells (14 x 35),

    168 smoke shells (14 x 12),

for each M. G. 1 150 pointed bullet with hardened steel core cartridges, half of which are tracers.

for **Pz. Kpfw. II:**

    300 explosive shells (5 x 60),

    300 armor-piercing shells (5 x 60),

for each 1 075 pointed bullet with hardened steel core cartridges, half of which are tracers.

Anlage 4

Führungszeichen.

Außer den Führungszeichen nach H. Dv. 472 werden folgende Flaggenzeichen angewandt:

		a) Ruhig gehalten:	b) Mehrfach hochgestoßen:	c) Geschwenkt:	d) Aus geöffnetem Turm nach unten gehalten:
1	Gelbe Flagge	Wir folgen!	-	Reihe!	-
2	Blaue Flagge	Doppelreihe!	Luken dicht!	Keil!	Luken auf!
3	Rote Flagge	Gefechtsbereitschaft!	Klar zum Gefecht!	Abwehrgeschütz bzw. feindl. Pz. Kpf. Wg. oder Artillerie angreifen! Breitkeil!	Klar zum Gefecht beendet oder Gefechtsbereitschaft beendet!
4	Rote und Gelbe Flagge	Stellung!	-	Linksum!	-
5	Blaue und Gelbe Flagge	Rechtsum!	-	-	-
6	Blaue und Rote Flagge	Volle Deckung!	-	Kehrt! – Marsch!	-
7	Führerwinkel zusammen mit Zeichen 1 bis 6	Führer hier!	Ganze Kompanie!	Eigene Panzer!	-
8	Ausfallflagge	Ausfall!	-	Hilfe erforderlich!	-

Siehe Ergänzung 1 im Anhang für den vollständigen Titel.

Appendix 4

Driving Signals.

In addition to the driving signals according to H. Dv. 472, the following flag signals shall be used:

		a) Kept steady:	b) Pushed up multiple times:	c) Swiveled:	d) From open turret held down:
1	Yellow Flag	We follow!	-	Column!	-
2	Blue Flag	Double column!	Close hatches!	Wedge!	Open the hatches!
3	Red Flag	Readiness for action!	Ready for combat!	Attack defensive gun or enemy tank or artillery!	'Ready for combat' finished! or 'readiness for action' finished!
4	Red and Yellow Flag	Position!	-	Inverted wedge!	-
5	Blue and Yellow Flag	Right, face!	-	Left, face!	-
6	Blue and Red Flag	Full cover!	-	Turn! - March!	-
7	Guide chevron together with signals 1 to 6	Commanders here!	-	Own tanks! Whole company!	-
8	Malfunction flag	Malfunction!	-	Help required!	-

See Supplement 1 in the Appendix for the full title.

[Leere Seite wie in Original H. Dv. 470/7.]

[Intentionally left blank as in the original H. Dv. 470/7.]

Anlage 5.
Ausführung der Flaggen.

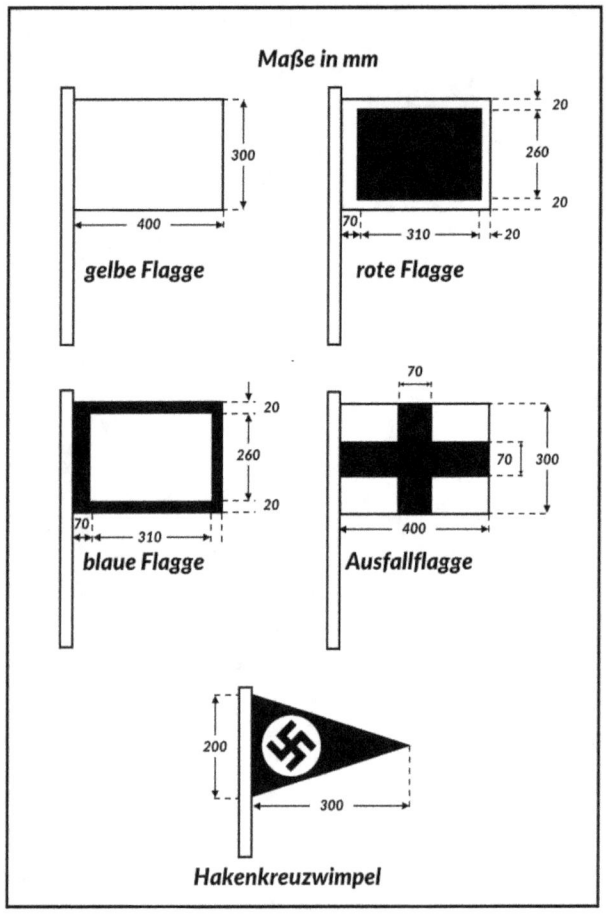

Appendix 5.
Design of Flags.

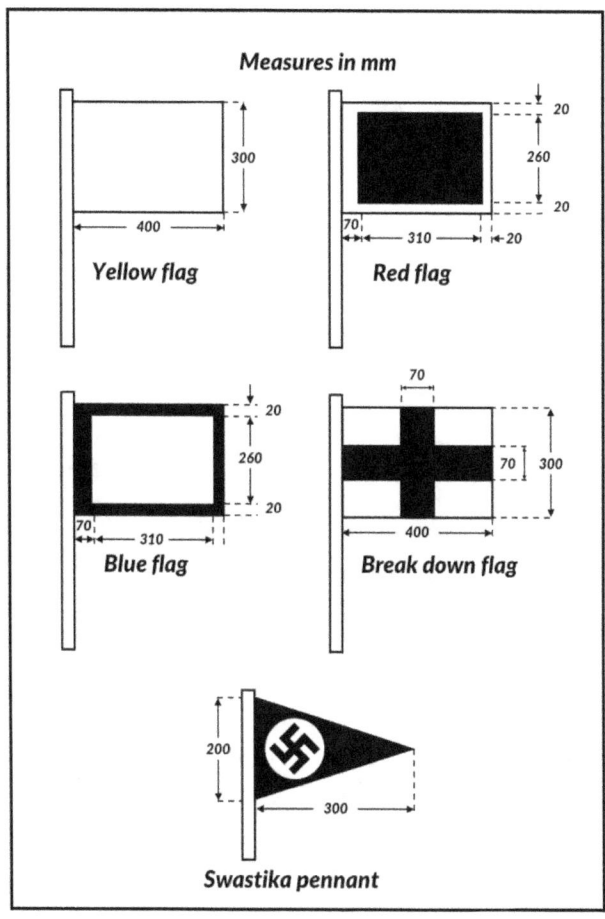

[Leere Seite wie in Original H. Dv. 470/7.]

[Intentionally left blank as in the original H. Dv. 470/7.]

Anlage 6

Erläuterung der Stoßlinie[156].

Die Bezeichnung von Kartenpunkten mit Hilfe der Stoßlinie dient zur Befehlsübermittlung, Erstattung von Meldungen und Leitung des Artilleriefeuers.

Zwei Kartenpunkte – möglichst Kirchtürme – im Bewegungsstreifen der Division werden auf der Karte miteinander verbunden; die Verbindungslinie muß in der Angriffsrichtung liegen. Auf dieser Linie wird eine cm-Einteilung vorgenommen, Nullpunkt etwa in Höhe der Ausgangsbasis der Division.

Die Bezeichnung eines bestimmten Punktes (Ziel) wird dadurch ermittelt, daß man von ihm eine Senkrechte auf die Stoßlinie fällt.

Seine Lage wird bestimmt:

    a) nach der Entfernung vom Nullpunkt der Stoßlinie bis zum Schnittpunkt der auf sie gefällten Senkrechten,

    b) nach der senkrechten Entfernung des Punktes von der Stoßlinie.

So erfolgt z. B. die Bezeichnung eines Ortes, der in Höhe des Punktes 9 (9 cm vom Nullpunkt) der Stoßlinie und 2,7 cm rechts von ihr liegt, im Funkspruch durch „9 rechts 2,7".

---

[156] Die Stoßlinie war eine Referenzlinie auf Karten, die es den Einheiten erlaubte im Gefecht relativ darauf zu verweisen. Dies ermöglichte eine einfache Orientierung und verhinderte, dass der Feind beim Abfangen der Funksprüche die Position zurückermitteln konnte.

Appendix 6
Explanation of the Axis Reference Line[157].

The designation of map points with help of the axis reference line is used for the transmission of orders, delivering reports and direction of artillery fire.

Two map points - if possible church towers - in the sector of movement[158] of the division are connected with each other on the map; the line of communication must lie in the direction of attack. A partitioning by centimeters is made on this line, with ground zero approximately level with the starting point of the division.

The designation of a certain point (target) is determined by a line running perpendicular to the axis reference line.

The position will be determined:

    a) based on the distance from ground zero on the axis reference line to the intersection with the perpendicular,

    b) based on the vertical distance of the point from the axis reference line.

For example, the designation of a location located at the height of point 9 (9 cm from zero) of the thrust line and 2.7 cm to the right of it is given in the radio message by "9 right 2.7".

---

[157] The axis reference line (German: "Stoßlinie" which literally translates to "thrust line") was a map reference line that allowed units to communicate their relative position in combat. This allowed for quick orientation and coordination, while it prevented the enemy from locating the units when intercepting the radio reports, unless the German thrust line was known.

[158] The literal translation of the German word "Bewegungsstreifen" would be "movement strip".

Das Ablesen erfolgt von Karten aller Maßstäbe einheitlich in cm. Bei Ausgabe der Stoßlinie ist grundsätzlich der Maßstab zu befehlen, nach dem gemeldet werden soll.

Erfolgt die Meldung nach einer anderen Karte, ist der Maßstab anzugeben. Notwendige Umrechnungen zum Übertragen des gemeldeten Punktes auf Karten anderer Maßstäbe sind durch den Empfänger vorzunehmen.

Um dem Feind das Abhören von Funksprüchen nach der Stoßlinie zu erschweren, wird auf Befehl der Division an verschiedenen Tagen der Anfang der Stoßlinie nicht mit Null, sondern mit einer anderen Zahl bezeichnet. Bei Knicken im Bewegungsstreifen der Division wird die Stoßlinie an den Knickpunkten neu bezeichnet. Hierbei ist als Anfangszahl der neuen Stoßlinie eine Zahl zu wählen, die so viel von den nahe gelegenen Zahlen der alten Stoßlinie abweicht, daß eine Verwechslung ausgeschlossen ist.

Reading from maps of all scales is done uniformly in centimeters. When issuing the axis reference line, the scale used for reporting must be given.

If the message is sent according to another map, the scale must be indicated. Necessary conversions to transfer the reported point to maps of other scales are to be carried out by the recipient.

In order to complicate the enemy's efforts to eavesdrop for radio reports using the axis reference line, the division can alternate the first number of the reference line from zero to another number on different days. In the case of bends in the sector of movement of the division, the reference line at the bends is renamed. The starting number of the new line is a number which differs so much from the nearby numbers of the initial line that confusion can be avoided.

Zeichen:[159]

Pendeln des Winkerstabes:
> Hier Infanterie-Zug- (Kompanie-) Führer!

Stillhalten des Winkerstabes:
> Halten! Hier Deckung!

Winkerstab in Feindrichtung gestoßen:
> Weiterfahren! Zielrichtung!

Geballte Faust:
> Panzerabwehrwaffe!

Gespreizte Hand:
> Infanterienest!

---

[159] Anmerkung: Dies war eine ausklappbare Seite. Dieser Text befand auf dem Innenteil von Seite 89 und die Signale, die sich nun auf Seite 90 befinden waren auf dem Außenteil. Um die Seitenzahlen wie im Original beizubehalten, haben wir in diesem Fall darauf verzichtet Seite 90 leer zu lassen und darauf Anhang 7 gedruckt.

Signals:[160]

Swinging of the signaling disk:

> This is Infantry Platoon (Company) Commander!

Keeping the signaling disk still:

> Hold it! Take cover!

Pointing the signaling disk in enemy direction:

> Keep moving! Direction of the target!

Clenched fist:

> Anti-tank weapon!

Splayed hand:

> Infantry position!

---

[160] Note this was a fold-out page with the text situated on the inner side of page 89 and with the corresponding signals (now page 90) on the outer side. To keep the page numbering with the original, we omitted to leave page 90 blank and instead printed Appendix 7 on it.

Anlage 7.
Winkertafel der Infanterie.

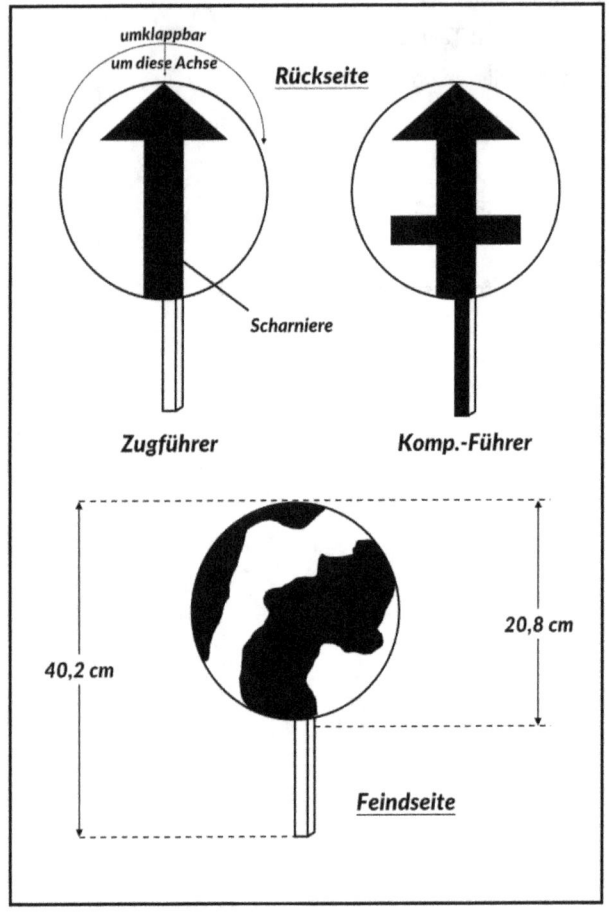

Appendix 7.
Signaling disk of the infantry.

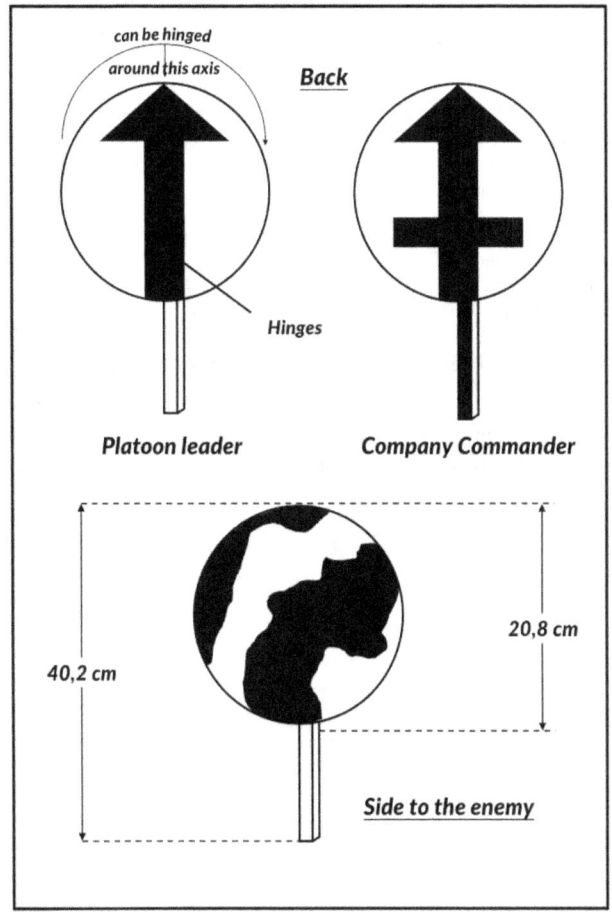

Anlage 8

Merkblatt über Bekämpfungsmöglichkeit von Panzersperren und Überwinden von Panzerhindernissen

I. Allgemeine Grundsätze.

1. **Man unterscheidet** Panzersperren und Hindernisse für Panzerkampfwagen.

    Panzersperren – künstliche geschaffene Hindernisse, die durch Kampfanlagen gesichert sind – werden gebildet durch Panzergräben, Schienen- und Gittersperren, Höcker- und Igelsperren, Panzerminen, Fallen und Straßensperren.

    Panzerhindernisse sind Waldungen, Trichterfelder, Steilhänge, Weinberge, Gewässer und Sümpfe.

2. Alle Panzersperren – außer Minen und Fallen – sind zu erkennen, Hindernisse oft erst durch Gefechtsaufklärung festzustellen. Ihre Art kann nach den Merkmalen festgestellt werden (siehe II).

    Aufklärung und **Erkundung von Einzelheiten** über Lage und Art der Sperren und Hindernisse vor dem Angriff sind für den Angriffserfolg der Panzerkampfwagen Vorbedingung.

Appendix 8

Pamphlet on how to engage[161] Tank Barriers and Overcoming of Tank Obstacles

I. General Principles.

1. **A distinction is made** between tank barriers and tank obstacles.

   Tank barriers - artificial obstacles created and secured by fighting structures - are formed by tank ditches, rail and grid barriers, dragon teeth and hedgehog barriers, [anti-]tank mines, traps and road barriers.

   Tank obstacles are forests, crater fields, steep slopes, vineyards, waters and swamps.

2. All tank barriers - except mines and traps - can be identified. Usually obstacles can only be identified by battle reconnaissance. Their category can be determined according to the characteristics (see II).

   A precondition to the success of the tank assault is the preceding **reconnaissance** and **investigation of details** in regard to the location and type of barriers and obstacles.

---

[161] The literal translation of the German word "Bekämpfungsmöglichkeit" is "combat/engagement possibilities".

3. Das **Überwinden** von Panzersperren und Panzerhindernissen ist nur selten ohne vorheriges Zerstören bzw. ohne den Einsatz von Hilfsmitteln möglich.

   Panzersperren sind in den meisten Fällen erst nach Zerstörung oder Schaffen von Gassen durch Panzerkampfwagen zu überwinden.

   Soweit Panzerhindernisse durch Panzerkampfwagen zu überwinden sind, wird deren Gefechtsstätigkeit dabei eingeschränkt. Meist ist Schaffen von Gassen oder Übergängen durch Pioniere erforderlich.

4. Zum Öffnen von Panzersperren und Hindernissen durch Zerstörung oder **Überbrückung** sind die **Mittel im Schwerpunkt zusammenzufassen sowie überraschend und schnell zur Wirkung zu bringen.**

   Nebelverwendung, Ausführung bei Nacht und Täuschen an anderer Stelle verschleiern dem Gegner die beabsichtigte Durchbruchsstelle; Angriff und Wirkung aller anderen Waffen auf breiter Front zersplittern seine Abwehr.

   Alle Arbeiten an Sperren und Hindernissen erfordern Ausschalten der feindlichen Waffenwirkung. Der Schwerpunkt der Waffenwirkung muß auf dem Feind hinter den Panzersperren an der Durchbruchsstelle liegen.

3. The **overcoming** of tank barriers and tank obstacles is only rarely possible without prior destruction or without the employment of aids.

   In most cases, tank barriers can only be overcome after their destruction or creation of lanes by tanks.

   If tank obstacles are to be overcome by tanks, their combat strength will be limited throughout this action. Usually the creation of lanes or transitions by engineers is required.

4. To overcome[162] tank barriers and obstacles by **destruction** or **bridging, equipment is gathered at the critical point**[163] and must be **brought into effect with surprise and speed**.

   The use of fog, night-time and by misleading the enemy through actions elsewhere, the intended penetration point can be concealed; the attack and effect of all other weapons on a broad front fragment the enemies defense.

   All work on barriers and obstacles requires the elimination of enemy weapons affecting this task. The main effort must concentrate on the enemy behind the tank barriers at the penetration point.

---

[162] The literal translation of the German word "Zum Öffnen", is "to open".

[163] From the German original "Schwerpunkt", designating the area on which the main effort should be concentrated. See also Schneider, Panzer Tactics, p. vi. Note there is a long, on-going discussion on how one could translate and conceptualize "Schwerpunkt" with different opinions found in various academic and military circles. This discussion is beyond the scope of this publication.

5. **Zerstörungsmittel** sind:

   Beschuß mit Artillerie und s. I. G.[164],

   Fliegerbomben,

   besonders Kampfmittel der Pioniere (Sprengladungen),

   Rammwirkung der Panzerkampfwagen.

   Hilfsmittel zur Überwindung sind:

   Faschinen und Behelfsmittel,

   Behelfsbrücken (Spurtafel[165]),

   Knüppelteppiche,

   Kriegsbrückengerät.

6. **Sprenggranaten** haben erst ab Kaliber 7,5 cm Wirkung. Zur Vermeidung von Trichterwirkung ist besonders bei größeren Kalibern mit Sprenggranaten o. V.[166] zu schießen. Direkter Beschuß mit Kampfwagenkanonen, schweren Flak auf Selbstfahrlafetten bringt rasche Wirkung auf Entfernungen bis 1 000 m.

   Gegen Minenfelder ist durch Gassenschießen mit Artillerie nur unter großem Munitionseinsatz Wirkung zu erreichen.

7. Einsatz von **Fliegerbomben** können die Artilleriewirkung erhöhen. Die entstehenden Trichter können zu neuen Hindernissen für Panzerkampfwagen werden.

---

[164] Es handelt sich hierbei um das 15-cm schwere Infanteriegeschütz 33 (s. I. G. 33). Oft wird dieses auch mit s. J. G. abgekürzt.

[165] Spurtafeln sind die Teile einer Pontonbrücke/Schwimmbrücke, die für die Räder bzw. Ketten der zu überquerenden Fahrzeuge gedacht sind.

[166] Ohne Verzögerung.

5. **Destructive agents** are:

   artillery fire and s. I. G.[167],

   aircraft bombs,

   destructive equipment of the engineers (explosive charges),

   ramming by tanks.

   Aids for overcoming barriers are:

   fascines and makeshift equipment,

   provisional [pontoon] bridges (treadway[168]),

   corduroy/log roads,

   military bridges.

6. **Explosive shells** are only effective from caliber 7.5 cm upwards. In order to avoid the cratering effect of large calibers, it is paramount to shoot with a non-delay fuze. Direct firing with vehicle guns, heavy anti-aircraft guns on self-propelled gun carriages bring near-immediate success at distances of up to 1 000 m.

   Against minefields, creating lanes with artillery is only effective when using large amounts of ammunition.

7. The employment of **aircraft bombs** can increase the artillery effect. The resulting craters can become new obstacles for tanks.

---

[167] This is the 15-cm heavy infantry support gun 33 (s. I. G. 33). This is often abbreviated as s. J. G..

[168] A treadways are the parts of a pontoon bridge which are intended for the wheels or tracks of the crossing vehicles.

8. **Sprengmittel** werden durch Pionierstoßtrupps oder durch Sondergerät der Panzertruppe angewendet. Einsatz von Pionierstoßtrupps bedingt stets Angriff der Panzerkampfwagen im Nachstoß; Einsatz von Sondergerät unter dem Schutz anderer Panzerkampfwagen läßt vielfach rasches Folgen der Masse der Panzerkampfwagen zum Angriff zu.

9. **Rammen mit Panzerkampfwagen** ist nur gegen leicht gebaute Sperren möglich, Rammen in ansteigenden Gelände meist zwecklos.

10. **Faschinen und Behelfsmittel** dienen zum Ausfüllen von Grabenstücken und Trichtern sowie von Winkeln[169] vor Steilmauern. Auf den Panzerkampfwagen können sie nur in begrenzter Menge mitgeführt werden.

11. **Spurtafelbrücken** dienen zum Überbrücken von Grabenstücken bis zu 5 m Breite.

12. **Knüppelteppiche** dienen zum Überwinden von Sumpfstrecken sowie schlüpfrigen, vereisten und felsigen Hängen.

13. **Kriegsbrückengerät** und Brückenlegerkampfwagen der Pioniere werden besonders an breiten Hindernissen eingesetzt. Der Einsatz von Brückengerät der Pioniere setzt vorheriges Bilden ausreichend gesicherter Brückenköpfe voraus. Brückenlegerkampfwagen können den Übergang auch in feindlicher Feuerwirkung herstellen,

---

[169] Hierbei ist eine Rampe gemeint.

8. **Explosives** are employed by engineer assault detachments or by special equipment of the armored troops. The employment of engineer assault detachments always requires the attack of the tanks in the follow-up thrust; the use of special equipment under the protection of other tanks often permits a rapid follow-up of the attack with a mass of armored units.

9. **Ramming with tanks** is only possible against lightly built barriers, while ramming in ascending terrain is usually pointless.

10. **Fascines and makeshift equipment** are used to fill trench sections and craters as well as ramps[170] in front of steep walls. They can only be carried in limited quantities on tanks.

11. **Treadway bridges** are used to bridge trench sections up to 5 m wide.

12. **Corduroy/log bridges are** used for overcoming swamp stretches as well as slippery, icy and rocky slopes.

13. **Military bridges** and bridge laying tanks of the engineers are used especially at wide obstacles. The employment of engineer bridging equipment requires the prior formation of sufficiently secured bridgeheads. Bridge-laying tanks can also create a crossing when subject to hostile fire,

---

[170] The German word "Winkel" translates to "angle", yet from the context it must be a ramp.

wobei Niederhalten der Panzerabwehr notwendig ist.

14. Das **Überwinden von Hindernissen** erfordert sorgfältige Ausbildung der Panzerfahrer, da jedes Hindernis eine besondere Fahrweise bedingt. Anweisungen bezüglich Fahrgeschwindigkeit und Fahrtrichtung sind auf Grund der Erkundungsergebnisse von Fall zu Fall zu geben.

II. Panzersperren.

1. Panzergräben.

Merkmale:

Taktisch: durchlaufend, meist geradlinig im Zuge von Widerstandslinien angelegt, durch Kampfstände gesichert und häufig an andere Sperren oder Hindernisse angelehnt, im Luftbild meist gut sichtbar, von der Erde aus bei guter Tarnung oft erst aus geringer Entfernung an den Erdaufwürfen erkennbar.

Kurze, durch aufgebrachte Erddecken getarnte Panzergräben dienen in scheinbaren Lücken als Panzerfallen, sie sind nicht zu erkennen.

Technisch:

Trockene Panzergräben:

Dreiecksgräben: mindestens 1,5 bis 2 m tief, 2,5 bis 7 m breit, mit Erdaufwürfen beiderseits (0,7 m hoch) oder feindwärts (bis 1 m

although suppressing the enemies anti-tank weapons remains necessary.

14. The **overcoming of obstacles** requires careful training of the tank drivers, since each obstacle requires a special driving style. Instructions regarding speed and direction are given on a case-by-case basis based on the reconnaissance reports.

II. Tank Barriers.

1. Tank Ditches.

Characteristics:

Tactical: continuous, mostly in a straight line in alignment with the lines of enemy resistance, secured by fighting positions and often leaned against other barriers or obstacles, usually well visible in the aerial view, from the ground if well camouflaged they are often only recognizable via the constructed earthworks from a short distance.

Short anti-tank ditches camouflaged by covers are employed in apparent gaps as tank traps, and cannot be identified.

Technically:

Dry tank ditches:

> *Triangular ditches*: at least 1.5 to 2 m deep, 2.5 to 7 m wide, with earthworks on both sides (0.7 m high) or towards the enemy (up to 1 m

hoch), teilweise mit Betonmauer an der rückwärtigen Grabenwand.

Überwinden nach Einschießen oder Sprengen der Steilwand (7,5 cm Kw. K.-Sprenggranate m. V.[171], Betonwand durch 21 cm-Granate oder Sprengladung), nach Auffüllen mit Faschinen bzw. Abstechen der rückwärtigen Grabenkrone[172] oder über Brückengerät.

Breite Gräben: mindestens 2 m tief, Breite oben 3,5 bis 7 m, an der Sohle 1,6 bis 2 m, rückwärtige Grabenwand steil, vielfach Betonwand, Erdaufwürfe beiderseits 0,3 bis 1 m.

Überwinden meist nur durch Einschießen der rückwärtigen Grabenwand aus nächster Nähe, durch Auffüllen mit Faschinen bzw. Erdreich oder über Brückengerät.

Nasse Panzergräben:

Dreieckgraben: bis zu 6 m tief, bis zu 12 m breit, meist symmetrische Keilform, rückwärtige Wand vereinzelt aus Beton. Durch Wasserfüllung oft weiche, zum mindesten schlüpfrige Grabenwand.

Überwinden durch Auffüllen mit Faschinen oder über Brückengerät.

Breite Gräben: mindestens 2 m tief, obere Breite 6 m und mehr, rückwärtige Grabenwand vielfach durch Beton oder Faschinenbau steil ausgeführt.

---

[171] mit Verzögerung(szünder).

[172] Die Grabenkrone ist das Pendant zur Grabensohle, es handelt sich um den oberen Teil des Grabens.

high), partly with concrete walls at the rear side of the trench.

Overcome after softening or blasting the steep wall (7.5 cm Kw. K. high-explosive shell with delay, concrete wall with a 21 cm shell or blasting charge), after filling with fascines or by cutting off rear top of the ditch[173] or by means of bridging equipment.

Wide trenches: at least 2 m deep, width at the top 3.5 to 7 m, at the bottom 1.6 to 2 m, rear ditch wall steep, often concrete wall, earthworks on both sides 0.3 to 1 m.

Mostly only *overcome* by firing at the rear wall of the trench at close range, by filling it with fascines or soil or by using bridging equipment.

Wet tank ditches:

Triangular ditch: up to 6 m deep, up to 12 m wide, mostly symmetrical wedge shape, rear wall occasionally made of concrete. Due to water often soft, or at least with a slippery trench wall.

Overcome by filling with fascines or by using bridging equipment.

Wide trenches: at least 2 m deep, upper width 6 m and more, rear trench wall often made steep by concrete or fascines.

---

[173] The German original notes "Abstechen der rückwärtigen Grabenkrone". "Abstechen" and "Grabenkrone" translates to "cutting off" and "ditch crown" respectively. Thus "Grabenkrone" refers to the open, top side of the ditch.

Überwinden meist nur über Brückengerät, bei geringer Tiefe auch nach Auffüllen mit Faschinen oder Behelfsmitteln.

Erkennbarkeit:

Gräben von mehr als 12 m Breite lassen auf schwach gewölbte Sohle des Grabens (parabolischer Querschnitt) schließen. Bei nicht befestigen Ufern sind Gräben bis 12 m als flache Gräben anzusprechen.

Nasse Gräben bis 12 m Breite mit betonierten oder sonst befestigten Böschungsflächen können spitze Gräben sein und sind bei klarem Wasser auch aus größeren Höhen durch dunkle Mittellinie erkennbar.

2. Schienen- und Gittersperren.

Merkmale:

Taktisch: fortlaufend, in kilometerlange Ausdehnung, in einfachem Gelände meist ohne wesentliche Richtungsänderung, stets in Verbindung mit Kampfanlagen. Da ungetarnt, weithin sichtbar von der Erde und aus der Luft.

Technisch:

Schienensperren: In Beton oder ohne Beton tief in den Boden gerade oder feingeneigt eingelassene Schienen (Eisenbahn-, U-, Doppel-T- und betongefüllte Doppel-U-Schienen), meist

Overcome mostly only via bridging equipment, at shallow depths also after filling with fascines or makeshift equipment.

Recognizability:

Trenches with a width of more than 12 m suggest a slightly curved trench bottom (parabolic cross-section). In the case of unfortified banks[174], trenches of up to 12 m are to be considered as flat trenches.

Wet trenches up to 12 m wide with concrete or otherwise paved embankment areas can be pointed trenches and, with clear water, can be recognized from greater heights by a dark center line.

2. Rail and Grid Barriers.

Characteristics:

Tactical: continuous, in kilometer-long extensions, in simple terrain, mostly without significant change of direction, always in connection with combat facilities. Since [they are] un-camouflaged, they remain visible from far away from the ground and from the air.

Technically:

Rail barriers: rails embedded in concrete or without concrete deep into the ground, straight or finely inclined (railway, U-, double-T and concrete-filled double U rails), usually

---

[174] The literal translation of the German word "Ufer", is "shore".

schachbrettartig mehrreihig (bis zu 7 Reihen) angeordnet. Schienen in wechselnder Höhe, Abstände und Zwischenräume 0,75 bis 1,50 m.

Überwinden einreihiger Sperren aus Eisenbahn- oder ungefüllten U-Schienen bei Anlauf mit 12 bis 15 km/std., nötigenfalls mit zweimaligem Gegenfahren umzudrücken; dabei mit Fahrzeugmitte gegen Schiene; Gleiskette darf keine Schiene berühren. Eine Schiene nach der andere umdrücken.

Stärkere einreihige und mehrreihige Schienensperren müssen durch andere Mittel zerstört werden.

Diese sind:

a) Schießen von Waffen mit Sprenggranaten von Kaliber 7,5 cm an aufwärts,

b) Gassensprengungen mittels Sondergeräts der Pz.-Pioniere (Abwurfvorrichtungen von Zerstörer Pz. Kpf. Wg.[175]),

c) Sprengungen durch Pioniere.

Gittersperren: in Beton oder durch Streben und Sporne im Boden verankerte, miteinander festverbundene Stahlgitter (Winkel-, U- und T-Eisenstücke in vernietetem oder gekuppeltem Zusammenbau) einreihig angeordnet. Höhe zwischen 1,5 und 2,5 m.

Überwinden erst nach Zerstörung möglich[176][.]

---

[175] Hierbei handelt es sich wohl um den Ladungsleger I auf Fahrgestell Panzerkampfwagen I.

[176] Da der Satz hier abschließt sollte wohl ein Punkt gesetzt werden. Dieser ist jedoch im Original nicht vorhanden.

arranged in several rows (up to 7 rows) like a chessboard. Rails in varying heights, distances and spaces 0.75 to 1.50 m.

Overcome single-row barriers made of railway or unfilled U-rails at a speed of 12 to 15 km/h. When necessary, knock over by driving against them two times; [use] the center of the vehicle against the rail; the caterpillar track must not touch the rail. Turn over one rail at a time.

Stronger single-row and multi-row rail stops must be destroyed by other means.

These are:

a) Firing of weapons with explosive shells of 7.5 cm caliber upwards,

b) Lane blasting using special equipment of armored engineers (throwing devices of destroyer Pz. Kpf. Wg.[177]),

c) Blasting by engineers.

Grid barriers: steel grids anchored to the ground in concrete or by struts and spurs (angled, U and T iron pieces in riveted or coupled assembly) arranged in a single row. Height between 1.5 and 2.5 m.

Overcoming only possible after destruction[178][.]

---

[177] This is likely the "Ladungsleger I" (charge layer I) on the chassis of the Panzerkampfwagen I.

[178] It is very likely that a period should be placed here, yet the original has none.

Zerstörung wie bei Schienensperren durch Sprenggranaten oder Sprengladung, hauptsächlich auf die deutlich erkennbaren Kreuzstücke und Kupplungen.

3. Höcker- und Igelsperren.

Merkmale:

Taktisch: Durchlaufend, meist den Bodenformen und vorhandenen Kampfanlagen angepaßt, oft in kilometerlanger Ausdehnung ein- oder mehrreihig angelegt. Trotz Tarnanstrichen von der Erde und aus der Luft gut sichtbar.

Technisch:

Hohle Höcker: (Tetraeder) Einzelhöcker etwa 1 m hoch, aus drei Eisenbetonstreben im Betonguß oben verbunden, durch Eisenbetonpfähle im Erdboden verankert und durch Grundplattenkreuz auf dem Boden gegen Umwerfen gesichert.

Überwinden mit Hilfe von Faschinen und Behelfsmitteln oder nach Zerstören einzelner Höcker, so daß Druchbruchsgasse frei. Zum Zerstören direkt gerichteter Beschuß mit Sprenggranaten ab 7,5 cm oder durch Sprengladung gegen Betonkopf des Einzelhöckers.

Massive Höcker: Einzelhöcker etwa 1 m hoch, aus Eisenbeton hergestellte und durch Grundplatten aus Eisenbeton miteinander verbunden oder mit tiefen Sockeln in der Erde befestigt.

Destruction as with rail barriers by explosive shells or explosive charges, mainly on the clearly visible cross pieces and couplings.

3. Dragon Teeth and Czech Hedgehogs.

Characteristics:

Tactical: Continuous, mostly adapted to the soil shapes and existing combat facilities, often in kilometer-long extension of one or several rows. Despite camouflage coatings they remain visible from the ground and from the air.

Technically:

Hollow dragon teeth: (Tetrahedron) single hump about 1 m high, made of three reinforced concrete struts connected at the top by concrete casting, anchored in the ground by reinforced concrete piles and secured against being knocked over by a base plate cross on the ground.

Overcome with the help of fascines and makeshift equipment or after destroying individual humps, so that breakthrough lane is free. To destroy, fire with explosive shells from 7.5 cm upwards or set explosive charges against the concrete head of the individual hump.

Solid dragon teeth: individual humps about 1 m high, made of reinforced concrete and connected to each other by reinforced concrete base plates or fixed in the ground with deep pedestals.

Überwinden erst nach Zerstören der Höcker für eine Gasse durch Sprengladungen an den Sockeln der Höcker oder durch Schaffen einer Brückenbahn (Auffüllen mit Faschinen und Behelfsmaterial, Anlegen von Spurtafeln zum Auffahren).

Eisenbetonigel: Einzeligel als dreibeiniger Eisenbetonständer mit hochragender Betonstrebe, der sich beim Gegenfahren in den Boden rammt und mit der aufbäumenden Stütze gegen das Fahrzeug klemmt. Höhe bis zu 1,5 m.

Überwinden erst nach Zerstören oder Fortziehen einzelner Igel. Zerstörung durch Sprengung oder direkten Beschuß des Igelkreuzstückes mit Sprenggranaten ab 7,5 cm auf Entfernungen bis 800 m.

Stahligel: Einzeligel aus Winkeleisen als Kreuz mit durchgehender Achse zusammengenietet oder geschweißt, rammt sich durch Gegenfahren in den Erdboden und fängt das Fahrzeug zangenartig ab; bis zu 1,80 m hoch.

Überwinden erst nach Zerstören oder Fortziehen einzelner Igel. Zerstören durch Sprengung oder Beschuß des Igelkreuzstückes mit Sprenggranaten ab 7,5 cm auf Entfernungen bis 800 m.

4. Panzerminen.

Mit dem Vorhandensein von Minen (Minenfeldern, Streuminen und Stabminen) ist in Verbindung mit Panzersperren und -hindernissen stets zu

Overcome only after creating a lane by destroying the humps with explosive charges at their bases or by creating a bridge (filling up with fascines and auxiliary material, creating track boards to drive up).

Reinforced concrete hedgehog: Single hedgehog as a three-legged reinforced concrete column with towering strut, which rams itself into the ground when driven against and clamps against the vehicle with the raised support. Height up to 1.5 m.

Only *overcome* after destruction or removal of individual hedgehogs. Destruction by blasting, or by applying direct fire on, the hedgehog crosspiece with explosive shells from 7.5 cm at distances of up to 800 m.

Steel hedgehog: Single hedgehog made of angle iron riveted together or welded as a cross with a continuous axis, rams itself into the ground by driving against it and catches the vehicle like tongs; up to 1.80 m high.

Only *overcome* after destruction or removal of individual hedgehogs. Destroy by blasting or firing at the hedgehog crosspiece with explosive shells from 7.5 cm at distances of up to 800 m.

4. Anti-Tank Mines.

The presence of mines (minefields, uncontrolled mines[179] and stick mines), in conjunction with tank barriers and obstacles, must always

---

[179] Literal translation of "Streumine" would be "stray mine". This term sees use as a 2nd translation by the TM 30-506 but can be misleading as pointed out by Nicholas Moran. The TM 30-506 notes that an uncontrolled mine is "not laid according to regular pattern" on p. 180.

rechnen. Sie sollen diese Anlagen in Breite und Tiefe ergänzen. Streuminen lassen sich rasch legen, während das Verlegen von Minenfeldern Zeit erfordert. Stabminen sind insbesondere an Hecken, Zäunen und in anderen Sperren, Streuminen an Engen und Wegen zu erwarten.

Minenfelder.

Merkmale:

Die Minen werden in 2 bis 3 Reihen mit Abstand von 25 bis 30 m hintereinander in durchlaufenden Gräben riegelweise (je 3 bis 5 Stück mit 1,5 bis 2 m Zwischenraum auf Luke zur vorderen Reihe) verlegt. Nach dem Verlegen werden die Gräben wieder zugeworfen und haben aus der Luft das Aussehen von Kabelgräben.

Erkennen auch offen verlegter Minen ist durch Luftaufklärung aus 400 m nicht möglich, durch Artilleriebeschuß (Einzelfeuer, dessen Lage und Wirkung gut zu beobachten sind) festzustellen.

Minensperren, in Gräben verlegt, durch Luftaufklärung wie Kabelgräben zu sehen.

Zerstörung:

Durch Artillerie: Schießen von Gassen durch erkannte Minenfelder, dabei Munitionsbedarf für eine *Gasse* von 20 bis 25 m *Breite* und 100 m *Tiefe* etwa 120 Schuß 21 cm-Wrf.[180] Oder etwa 400 Schuß s. F. H.[181] oder etwa 400 Schuß s. I. G.[182] (nur im Ausnahmefall).

---

[180] Die Abkürzung Wrf. steht für Werfer, allerdings ist wohl der 21-cm-Mörser 16 auch Langer 21-cm-Mörser genannt gemeint, da der Nebelwerfer 42 für 1941 nicht in Frage kommt, ebenso verfügte die Wehrmacht zu diesem Zeitpunkt über keinen 21 cm Granatwerfer. Wichtig: Dieser „Mörser" war eine schwere Feldhaubitze, die Termini „Mörser" und „Granatwerfer" haben heute eine andere Bedeutung.

[181] Es handelt es sich hierbei um die schwere Feldhaubitze 18 mit dem Kaliber 15 cm.

[182] Es handelt sich hierbei um das 15-cm schwere Infanteriegeschütz 33 (s. I. G. 33) – Anmerkung oft wird dieses auch mit s. J. G. abgekürzt.

be reckoned with. They are intended to supplement these defenses in width and depth. Uncontrolled mines can be laid quickly, while laying minefields takes time. Stick mines are to be expected along hedges, fences and other barriers, and uncontrolled mines at narrow passages and paths.

Minefields.

Characteristics:

The mines are laid in 2 to 3 rows with a distance of 25 to 30 m behind each other in continuous trenches (3 to 5 each with 1.5 to 2 m space between each row on the hatch to the front row). After laying, the trenches are thrown in again and have the appearance of cable trenches from the air.

Detection of uncovered mines is not possible by air reconnaissance above 400 m, but can be detected by artillery fire (single fire, whose position and effect can be observed well).

Mine barriers laid in trenches, seen through aerial reconnaissance, appear like cable trenches.

Destruction:

By artillery: firing lanes through recognized minefields, ammunition requirement for a *lane of* 20 to 25 m *width* and 100 m *depth* about 120 shots 21 cm Wrf.[183]. Or about 400 rounds s. F. H.[184] or about 400 rounds s. I. G.[185] (only in exceptional cases).

---

[183] The abbreviation "Wrf." stands for "Werfer", but it is likely 21 cm Mörser 16 also called Langer 21 cm Mörser, because the Nebelwerfer 42 for 1941 is out of the question, also the Wehrmacht did not have a 21 cm mortar (called "Granatwerfer") at that time. Note although "Mörser" means "mortar", yet in this case it was a heavy howitzer, the German words "Mörser" and "Granatwerfer" have a different meaning in today's German.

[184] This is the schwere Feldhaubitze 18 (heavy field howitzer 18) with the caliber 15 cm.

[185] This is the 15-cm schwere Infanteriegeschütz 33 (s. I. G. 33 - heavy infantry gun 33) - note this is often abbreviated with s. J. G. in German documents.

Die besten Erfolgsaussichten bietet der 21 cm-Mörser.

Durch Pioniere: Schaffen von Gassen nach dem üblichen Verfahren (Spüren, Sprengen, Bezeichnen).

Überwindbarkeit durch Panzerkampfwagen:

Erst nach Schaffen von Gassen in Breite von mindestens 5 m, beiderseits bezeichnet. Durchfahren auf den Trichterfeldern am besten durch die Trichter selbst, falls diese nicht zu groß (vgl. III, 2).

5. Fallen.

Merkmale:

Taktisch: Durch Tarnung auch aus naher und nächster Entfernung nicht oder nur schwer erkennbare Gräben und Gruben, in die der Panzerkampfwagen bei Befahren der Tarnabdeckung hineinsackt, ohne sich mit eigener Kraft wieder herausarbeiten zu können. Meist in Lücken zwischen Sperren und Hindernissen oder in Engen angelegt; daher ist an solchen Stellen durch gründliche Luftbildererkundung danach zu suchen.

Technisch: Grabenstrecken oder Einzelgruben von mindestens 2 m Tiefe mit nahezu senkrechten Wänden und mindestens 4 m Durchmesser der Länge und Breite nach, durch sorgfältig aufgebrachte, für Menschen meist tragfähige Abdeckung getarnt.

The 21 cm field howitzer offers the best chances of success.

By engineers: Creation of lanes according to the usual procedure (detecting, blasting, marking).

Surmountability by tanks:

Only after creation of alleys in width of at least 5 m, marked on both sides. Drive through the crater fields, ideally into the craters themselves if they are not too large (compare III, 2).

5. Traps.

Characteristics:

Tactical: Due to camouflage ditches and pits - into which tanks slump when driving over and often are unable to escape by through their own power - are difficult to recognize even from close and proximate distances. Usually set in gaps between barriers and obstacles or in narrow places; therefore, such places must be identified by thorough aerial photography reconnaissance.

Technical: Trench sections or individual pits of at least 2 m depth with almost vertical walls and at least 4 m diameter in length and width, camouflaged by carefully applied cover, which is usually load-bearing for humans.

Überwinden – soweit Umfahren möglich ist – wie Panzergräben. Durch Entfernen der Tarnabdeckung für eigene Panzerkampfwagen kennzeichnen!

6. Straßensperren.

Merkmale:

Taktisch: Meist an Engstellen von Straßen und Wegen, wo Ausweichen oder Umfahren nicht möglich ist, errichtet. Meist durch Anlage hinter Kurven oder Höhen erst aus geringer Entfernung erkennbar. Umgebung, soweit befahrbar, vielfach durch Minen oder Fallen gefährdet.

Technisch:

Gittersperren: Stahlgitter oder herablaßbare Stahltore in ganzer Straßenbreite, vornehmlich in Brückenpfeilern oder zwischen starken Hausmauern angebracht.

Überwinden nach Zerstören durch Sprengung oder Beschuß der Schienenverbindungen bzw. Kupplungen mit Sprenggranaten ab 7,5 cm aus naher und mittlerer Entfernung.

Schrankensperren: Betongefüllte Stahlschranken von knapp 3 m Sperrweite zwischen meterstarken und meterhohen Eisenbetonpfeilern.

Überwinden nach Zerstören durch Sprengung oder Beschuß der Stahlschranken mit Sprenggranaten ab 7,5 cm aus naher Entfernung.

Overcome - as far as bypassing is possible - just as tank ditches. Mark by removing the camouflage cover for your own tanks!

6. Roadblocks.

Characteristics:

Tactical: Usually built at narrow points of roads and paths where avoidance or bypassing is not possible. Usually only recognizable from a short distance due to the installation behind curves or heights. Surroundings, if passable, often endangered by mines or traps.

Technically:

Grid barriers: Steel grids or lowerable steel gates across the entire width of the road, mainly in bridge piers or between strong house walls.

Overcome after destruction by blasting or direct fire of the rail connections or couplings with explosive shells of 7.5 cm and up, from close and medium distance.

Gate barriers: Concrete-filled steel barriers of almost 3 m width between meter-thick and meter-high reinforced concrete piers.

Overcome after destruction by blasting or fire of the steel barriers with explosive shells of 7.5 cm and up from close range.

Betonklotzsperren: Betongefüllte Betonröhren von etwa 1 m Durchmesser und 1 m Höhe mit längsgebetteter Stahlschiene, die als Schienensperre hervorragt; oder meterstarke Betonklötze, im Erdreich versenkt. Entweder als vollkommene Sperre oder schachbrettartig mit knappen Durchlässen, die minengefährdet sind, angeordnet.

Überwinden nach Zerstören durch Sprengung oder Beschuß mit Sprenggranaten größeren Kalibers.

Schienensperren: Meist in Verbindung mit durchlaufenden Schienensperren angelegt. Über Bauart, Zerstören und Überwinden siehe II, 2.

Seilsperren: Zwischen festen Betonsockeln gespannte starke Stahlseile, die niedrig gespannt, durch Panzerkampfwagen III und IV überfahren, sonst nur durch Sprengung geöffnet werden können.

Baumsperren: Quer zur Straße in dichtem Gewirr gefällte Bäume, untereinander oft verdrahtet und durch Minen gefährdet.

Überwinden von Baumsperren durch Auseinanderreißen oder Artilleriebeschuß. Vorhandensein von Minen ist vorher zu prüfen.

Barrikaden: Beschwertes Behelfsmaterial (steingefüllte, umgestürzte Wagen, Baumstämme, Pflastersteinwälle, Anschlagsäulen) in beliebiger Zusammenstellung.

Concrete block barriers: Concrete-filled concrete pipes of about 1 m diameter and 1 m height with longitudinally embedded steel rail protruding as a rail barrier; or meter-thick concrete blocks, sunk into the ground. Either arranged as a perfect barrier or like a chessboard with narrow passages which are endangered by mines.

Overcome after destruction by blasting or shell fire with larger caliber explosive shells.

Rail barriers: Usually used in conjunction with continuous rail barriers. About construction, destruction and overcoming see II, 2.

Rope barriers: Strong steel ropes tensioned between fixed concrete pedestals, which are passed over by Panzerkampfwagen III and IV with low tension, otherwise they can only be opened by blasting.

Tree barriers: Trees felled across the road in dense tangle, often wired together and endangered by mines.

Overcome tree barriers by tearing them apart or by exposing it to artillery fire. The presence of mines must be checked beforehand.

Barricades: Weighted auxiliary material (stone-filled, overturned wagons, tree trunks, paving stone walls, stop columns) in any combination.

Überwinden in den meisten Fällen durch Breschefahren von Panzerkampfwagen, Brescheschießen von Artillerie, sonst Einsatz von Pionieren.

Minensperren: Riegel von 3 bis 5 Minen schachbrettartig in 6 bis 8 Reihen hintereinander mit etwa 2 m Abstand von Reihe zu Reihe. Die Minen sind in die Straßendecke eingegraben und getarnt.

Zerstören: Durch Beschuß (siehe Minenfelder).

Beseitigen: Durch Pioniere nach dem üblichen Verfahren.

III. Hindernisse.

1. Waldungen.

Wälder sind vielfach auch außerhalb von Schneisen und Wegen durch Panzerkampfwagen zu durchfahren. Enger, starker Baumbestand sowie dichtes Unterholz erschwert dies.

Wald mit *Stämmen unter* 25 cm Durchmesser wird durch Panzerkampfwagen III und IV durchfahren. Dabei wird die Geschwindigkeit herabgesetzt.

Durch Wald mit *Stämmen über* 25 cm Durchmesser und so dicht, daß der Panzerkampfwagen gleich 2 Bäumen nehmen muß, können sich Panzerkampfwagen III und IV nur durchnagen.

Overcome in most cases by breaching with tanks, destruction by artillery fire, otherwise by committing engineers.

Mine barriers: Bars of 3 to 5 mines checkered in 6 to 8 rows one behind the other with a distance of about 2 m from row to row. The mines are dug into the road surface and camouflaged.

Destroy: By bombardment (see minefields).

Eliminate: By engineers according to the usual procedure.

III. Obstacles.

1. Woodlands.

Forests can often also be crossed by tanks outside of aisles and paths. This is made more difficult by a dense, strong tree population and dense undergrowth.

Forests with *trunks less than* 25 cm in diameter can be crossed by Panzerkampfwagen III and IV. This reduces their speed.

Through forests with *trunks over* 25 cm diameter and so dense that the tanks must hit 2 trees, can only be gnawed[186] through by Panzerkampfwagen III and IV.

---

[186] From the German "durchnagen", a word usually used when describing the biting action of a rodent.

Einzelne Bäume (Kiefern) bis 50 cm Durchmesser können durch Panzerkampfwagen III und IV umgebrochen werden.

Panzerkampfwagen I und II können durch eigene Kraft stärkeren Baumbestand nicht durchfahren.

2. Trichterfelder.

Trichterfelder sind Hindernisse, die ein Durchfahren von Panzerkampfwagen verhindern können und die Geschwindigkeit beim Überqueren wesentlich herabsetzen können.

Trichterfelder mit Trichtern, deren Durchmesser der Länge des Panzerkampfwagens entspricht und eine Böschung von etwa 45° haben, sind in der Regel durch Panzerkampfwagen nicht zu überwinden, wenn die Stegbreite zwischen den Trichtern die halbe Spurbreite des Panzerkampfwagens und mehr beträgt; die Überschreitbarkeit hängt wesentlich auch von der Bodenbeschaffenheit ab (trocken, naß, Lehm, Sand).

Durch Faschinen und Behelfsmittel können durch nicht zu überwindende Trichterfelder Übergänge geschaffen werden.

3. Steilhänge.

Steilhänge mit hoher Böschung sind durch Panzerkampfwagen nicht zu überwinden. Bei niedrigen Böschungen kann das Überqueren durch Brückenleger ermöglicht werden.

Individual trees (pines) up to 50 cm in diameter can be broken down by Panzerkampfwagen III and IV.

Panzerkampfwagen I and II cannot pass through stronger trees by their own power.

2. Crater Fields.

Crater fields are obstacles that can prevent tanks from passing through and can significantly reduce the speed when crossing.

Crater fields with craters whose diameter corresponds to the length of the tank and which have an embankment of about 45°, are generally not to be overcome by tanks if the distance between the craters corresponds to half the track width of the tank or more; the traversability depends on the condition of the ground (dry, wet, loam, sand).

Crater fields which cannot be overcome, can be traversed with fascines and makeshift means.

3. Steep Slopes.

Steep slopes with high embankments cannot be overcome by tanks. On low embankments, crossing can be made possible by bridge layers.

4. Weinberge.

Steile Weinberge mit hohen Steinmauern sind durch Panzerkampfwagen nicht, andere leicht zu überwinden.

5. Gewässer und Sümpfe (Wasserhindernisse).

Man unterscheidet Wasserläufe mit und ohne Anstauungen, Sümpfe und Überschwemmungen. Vielfach sind Wasserhindernisse durch Kampfanlagen geschützt, Überschwemmungen (zum großen Teil im Marsch- und Polderland) in Verbindung mit Befestigungen vorgenommen.

Überwinden breiter Wasserläufe (vgl. auch II, 1) sowie ausgedehnter Sümpfe und Überschwemmungen ist nur nach Schaffen besonderer Übergänge möglich. Der Einsatz dieser Mittel setzt eingehende Erkundung voraus, die sich zu erstrecken hat auf Beschaffenheit der Ufer (steil, flach, fest, morastig), die Wassertiefe und die Art des Untergrundes (fest, weich) sowie auf Annäherungsmöglichkeiten an die Übergangsstellen. Fest zugefroren können nicht zu breite Wasserhindernisse vielfach überschritten werden; die Tragfähigkeit des Eises kann durch Auflegen langer Bretter quer zur Fahrtrichtung erhöht werden.

Mittel zum Überwinden von Wasserhindernissen sind Faschinen, Baumstämme und andere Behelfsmittel. Für breitere Wasserläufe ist Brückengerät einzusetzen.

[Hier endet die H. Dv. 470/7.]

4. Vineyards.

Steep vineyards with high stone walls are not easy to overcome by tanks. Others are easily overcome.

5. Waters and Marshes (Water Obstacles).

A distinction is made between watercourses with and without dams, swamps and floods. In many cases, water obstacles are protected by combat facilities, and floods (mostly in marsh and polder land) are used in conjunction with fortifications.

Overcoming wide watercourses (compare also II, 1) as well as extensive swamps and floods is only possible after creating special crossings. The employment of these require detailed reconnaissance, which must cover the nature of the banks (steep, shallow, firm, boggy), the depth of the water and the type of subsoil (firm, soft), as well as the possibility of approaching the crossing points. When frozen, water obstacles that are not too wide can be crossed in many cases; the load-bearing capacity of the ice can be increased by laying long boards across the direction of travel.

Means of overcoming water hazards are fascines, tree trunks and other makeshift means. Bridging equipment should be used for wider watercourses.

[Here ends the H. Dv. 470/7.]

Ergänzung 1: Liste der Vorschriften mit Titel

Heeresdruckvorschriften

H. Dv. 130/2a: Ausbildungsvorschrift für die Infanterie: Heft 2a: Die Schützenkompanie.

H. Dv. 225/2: Zielbau und Sicherheitsbestimmungen für Schießen aller Waffen.- Teil 2: Sicherheitsbestimmungen.

H. Dv. 421/4: Ausbildungsvorschrift für die Nachrichtentruppe (A.V.N.). Heft 4: Funkdienst im Heer.

H. Dv. 470/1: Ausbildungsvorschrift für die Panzertruppe. Heft 1: A. Leitsätze für die Erziehung und Ausbildung im Heere. B. Ausbildungsziele für die Einzelausbildung der Panzertruppe.

H. Dv. 470/5b: Ausbildungsvorschrift für die Panzertruppe (A. V. Pz.) Heft 5b Die Ausbildung am Panzerkampfwagen II (2 cm) Sonderkraftfahrzeug 121 (Sd. Kfz. 121).

H. Dv. 470/5d: Ausbildungsvorschrift für die Panzertruppe (A. V. Pz.) Heft 5d Die Ausbildung am Panzerkampfwagen IV, Sonderkraftfahrzeug 161 (Sd. Kfz. 161).

H. Dv. 472: Kraftfahrvorschrift für alle Waffen.

Dienstvorschriften

D 237: Hierbei handelt es sich entweder um einen Druckfehler oder eine nicht aufgeführte Dienstvorschrift. Während unserer Recherchen im Bundesarchiv in diversen Dokumenten wie den Kriegssoll an Vorschriften und Verzeichnissen zu Dienstvorschriften konnten wir keinen Eintrag zu D 237 finden. Ebenso enthält die H. Dv. 470/6: Die leichte Kompanie (1940) keinen Verweis auf die D 237, obwohl die leichten Kompanien ebenso mit Panzerkampfwagen II ausgestattet waren. Dies könnte ein Hinweis darauf sein, dass die Dienstvorschrift 1940 noch nicht existent war. Allerdings ist auch in der H. Dv. 470/22a Schulschießübungen vom Panzerkampfwagen II (1942) kein Verweis enthalten.

In der H. Dv. 1/8: Kriegssoll (Heer) an Vorschriften. Heft 8: Panzertruppe - Feldheer vom 1. 10. 1943 konnten wir leider keinen Eintrag für die D 237 finden.[187]

---

[187] BArch, RH 1/384: H. Dv. 1/8 Kriegssoll (Heer) an Vorschriften – Heft 8 – Panzertruppe-Feldheer, Oktober 1943.

Supplement 1: List of regulations with title

Army Regulations[188]

H. Dv. 130/2a: Training Regulations for the Infantry: Issue 2a: The Rifle Company.

H. Dv. 225/2: Target Construction and Safety Requirements for Firing of all Weapons - Issue 2: Safety Requirements.

H. Dv. 421/4: Training Regulation for the Signal Corps. Issue 4: Radio Service in the Army.

H. Dv. 470/1: Training Regulations for the Armored Troops. Issue 1: A. Guidelines for Army Education and Training. B. Training Objectives for the Individual Training of the Armored Troops.

H. Dv. 470/5b: Training Regulations for the Armored Troops. Issue 5b Training on the Panzerkampfwagen II (2 cm) Sonderkraftfahrzeug 121 (Sd. Kfz. 121).

H. Dv. 470/5d: Training Regulations for the Armored Troops. Issue 5d Training on the Panzerkampfwagen IV, Sonderkraftfahrzeug 161 (Sd. Kfz. 161).

H. Dv. 472: Motor Vehicle Regulations for all Weapons.

Service regulations

D 237: It is possible that this document code is a printing error or a non-listed service regulation. During our research in the German Federal Archive in various documents like the Authorized War Inventory[189] of Regulations and directories of service regulations we could find no reference to D 237. Similarly, the H. Dv. 470/6: The Light Company (1940) also makes no reference to D 237, although this unit was also equipped with the Panzerkampfwagen II. It is possible that the regulation in question was not yet in print in 1940 and that the number was being reserved. Yet, in H. Dv. 470/22a Live Firing Training with the Panzerkampfwagen II (1942) there is also no reference to this regulation.

Equally, in the H. Dv. 1/8: Authorized War Inventory (Army) of Regulations. Issue 8: Armored Troops – Field Army from 1943 no reference to D 237 was found[190].

---

[188] The literal translation of the "Heeresdruckvorschrift" would be "Army Print Regulation".

[189] "Kriegssoll" literally translated means "war debit".

[190] BArch, RH 1/384: H. Dv. 1/8 Kriegssoll (Heer) an Vorschriften: Heft 8. Panzertruppe-Feldheer, Oktober 1943.

Eine weitere mögliche Quelle für die Antwort wäre die H. Dv. 470/5b: Ausbildung am Panzerkampfwagen II (2 cm), jedoch findet sich in diesem Werk auch kein Verweis auf D 237[191].

Basierend auf dem Verzeichnis der waffentechnischen D+-Vorschriften vom 15. Oktober 1941 gehen wir davon aus, dass es sich bei D 237 wohl um eine Dienstvorschrift für die 2 cm Kanone des Panzerkampfwagen II handeln könnte[192]. Da es sich bei D 223/1+ um ein Werk über eine 3,7 cm Bewaffnung eines Panzers handelt. Das Problem hier ist jedoch, dass es sich bei den „+" Vorschriften um **geheime** außerplanmäßige Vorschriften handelt, wohingegen es sich bei den D-Vorschriften bloß um außerplanmäßige Vorschriften handelt, die jedoch nicht geheim sind.

Im Katalog der Druckvorschriften der ehemaligen Wehrmacht, zusammengestellt durch das Bundesminsiterium der Verteidigung der Bundesrepublik Deutschlands in 1960, findet sich auch kein Eintrag zur D 237[193].

D 603: Kraftfahrgerät Krupp-Traktor.

D 613/2: Vorläufige Anweisungen für die Ausbildung von Panzereinheiten. Teil 2: Anweisung für die Durchführung der Schießausbildung von Panzerkampfwagen bei der leichten Panzer-Kp.

D 613/7: Vorläufige Anweisungen für die Ausbildung von Panzereinheiten, Teil 7: Schießübungen vom Panzerkampfwagen II (2 cm) Sd. Kfz. 121.

D 613/9: Vorläufige Anweisungen für die Ausbildung von Panzer- und Panzerspäheinheiten, Teil 9: Vorbereitende Übungen für das Schießen von Panzerfahrzeugen und Schießausbildungsbehelfe.

D 613/10: Vorläufige Anweisungen für die Ausbildung von Panzer- und Panzerspäheinheiten, Teil 10: Panzerschießvorschrift: Lehre für das Schießen von Panzerfahrzeugen.

D 613/12: Vorläufige Anweisungen für die Ausbildung von Panzereinheiten. Teil 12: Anweisung für den Funkverkehr der Panzerverbände.

D 613/14: Vorläufige Anweisungen für die Ausbildung von Panzereinheiten. Teil 14: Schießübungen von Panzerkampfwagen IV (7,5 cm), Sd. Kfz. 161.

---

[191] H. Dv. 470/5b: Ausbildungsvorschrift für die Panzertruppe. Heft 5b: Die Ausbildung am Panzerkampfwagen II (2 cm) Sonderkraftfahrzeug 121 (Sd. Kfz. 121), 1939.

[192] BArch, RH 8/5912: Verzeichnis der waffentechnischen D+-Vorschriften, S. 6.

[193] BMVtg: Katalog der Druckvorschriften der ehemaligen deutschen Wehrmacht – Teil 1 Heer, Bonn, 1960, S. 119.

Another source that could provide an answer would be H. Dv. 470/5b: Training on the Panzerkampfwagen II (2 cm), yet in this publication there is also no reference to D 237[194].

Based upon the Directory of Weapons Technology D+-Regulations from the 15th October 1941, we assume that D 237 might be a regulation specifying the use of the 2 cm cannon used by the Panzerkampfwagen II[195]. Since D 223/1+ is a publication about a 3.7 cm gun of a tank. The problem with this hypothesis remains that the "+" symbol denominates these service regulations as **secret** unscheduled regulations, while "D" refers to service regulations that are just unscheduled yet not classified as secret.

Additionally, D 237 does not appear in the Catalogue of Druckvorschriften of the former Wehrmacht compiled in 1960 by the West-German Defense Ministry[196].

D 603: Motor Vehicle Krupp Tractor.

D 613/2: Preliminary Instructions for the Training of Armor Units. Issue 2: Instruction for the Execution of the Training in Firing of Tanks of the Light Tank Company.

D 613/7: Preliminary Instructions for the Training of Tank Units, Issue 7: Firing Practice from the Panzerkampfwagen II (2 cm) Sd. Kfz. 121.

D 613/9: Preliminary Instructions for the Training of Tank and Armored Reconnaissance Units, Issue 9: Preparatory Exercises for the Firing of Armored Vehicles and Firing Training Aids.

D 613/10: Preliminary Instructions for the Training of Tank and Armored Reconnaissance Units, Issue 10: Tank Firing Regulations: Guideline for the Firing with Armored Vehicles.

D 613/12: Preliminary Instructions for the Training of Armor Units. Issue 12: Instructions for the Radio Communication of Tank Units.

D 613/14: Preliminary Instructions for the Training of Armor Units. Issue 14: Firing Practice of Panzerkampfwagen IV (7.5 cm), Sd. Kfz. 161.

---

[194] H. Dv. 470/5b: Ausbildungsvorschrift für die Panzertruppe. Heft 5b: Die Ausbildung am Panzerkampfwagen II (2 cm) Sonderkraftfahrzeug 121 (Sd. Kfz. 121), 1939.

[195] BArch, RH 8/5912: Verzeichnis der waffentechnischen D+-Vorschriften, S. 6.

[196] BMVtg: Katalog der Druckvorschriften der ehemaligen deutschen Wehrmacht – Teil 1 Heer, Bonn, 1960, S. 119.

D 637: Unsere Recherche im Bundesarchiv hat leider keinen Namen für die D 637 zutage gefördert. Allerdings fanden wir Titel für eine D 637/1+ und D 637/2+ im Verzeichnis der geheimen außerplanmäßigen Heeres-Vorschriften (D+) vom 1. März 1937, welches im Januar 1938 ergänzt wurde.

Anmerkung die beiden Einträge D 637/1+ und D 637/2+ wurden ins Verzeichnis eingeklebt, vermutlich mit der Ergänzung vom Januar 1938[197]. Das Problem hier ist jedoch, dass es sich bei den „+" Vorschriften um **geheime** außerplanmäßige Vorschriften handelt, wohingegen es sich bei den D-Vorschriften bloß um außerplanmäßige Vorschriften handelt, die jedoch nicht geheim sind.

D 637/1+: Vorläufige Gerätebeschreibung und Bedienungsanweisung zum Fahrgestell des Panzerkampfwagen II (2 cm) (Sd. Kfz. 121). 25. 2. 37.

D 637/2+: Vorläufige Gerätebeschreibung und Bedienungsanweisung zum Fahrgestell des Panzerkampfwagen II (2 cm) (Sd. Kfz. 121) mit Beladeplan. 1. 4. 37.

Ebenso konnten wir in der H. Dv. 1/8: Kriegssoll (Heer) an Vorschriften. Heft 8: Panzertruppe - Feldheer vom 1. 10. 1943 konnten wir leider keinen Eintrag für die D 637 finden, wohingegen sich sieben Einträge mit anderen Ziffern für den Panzerkampfwagen II finden lassen[198].

D 651/1: Panzerkampfwagen II (2 cm) (Sd. Kfz. 121). Gerätebeschreibung und Bedienungsanweisung zum Fahrgestell.

D 651/2: Der Panzerkampfwagen II (2 cm) Sd. Kfz. 121) Ausführung A Fahrgestell Nr.20001 bis 23000 Teil 2: Ersatzteilliste.

D 653/1: Panzerkampfwagen IV (Sd. Kfz. 161). Ausführung A bis F. Gerätebeschreibung und Bedienungsanweisung zum Fahrgestell.

D 653/9: Der Panzerkampfwagen IV (7.5 cm) (VsKfz. 622) Ausführung A bis D Fahrgestell Nr. 80000 bis 80750 Beladeplan, 10.1.1939.

---

[197] BArch, RH 8/5909: Verzeichnis der geheimen außerplanmäßigen Heeres-Vorschriften (D+), März 1937 / Januar 1938, S. 16.

[198] BArch, RH 1/384: H. Dv. 1/8: Kriegssoll (Heer) an Vorschriften: Heft 8. Panzertruppe-Feldheer, Oktober 1943, S. 50.

D 637: Sadly, during our search in the German Military Archive D 637 could not be found. Nevertheless, we did find two documents that appear similar in code: D 637/1+ and D 637/2+ in the Directory of the secret unplanned Army-Regulations (D+) from 1st March 1937, which was updated in January 1938.

Note the two entries D 637/1+ and D 637/2+ were glued in paper slips, likely with the amendment from January 1938[199]. The problem remains that the "+" symbol indicates **secret** unscheduled regulations, while "D" refers to unscheduled regulations that are not classified as secret.

D 637/1+: Preliminary Equipment Description and Instruction Manual for the Chassis of the Panzerkampfwagen II (2 cm) (Sd. Kfz. 121). 25. February 37.

D 637/2+: Preliminary Equipment Description and Instruction Manual for the Chassis Panzerkampfwagen II (2 cm) (Sd. Kfz. 121) with Loading Plan. 1. April 37.

Equally, we could find no entry of the D 637 in the H. Dv. 1/8: Authorized War Inventory (Army) of Regulations. Issue 8: Armored Troops – Field Army from the 1st October 1943. Although seven other documents can be found referring to the Panzerkampfwagen II[200].

D 651/1: Panzerkampfwagen II (2 cm) (Sd. Kfz. 121). Equipment Description and Operating Instructions for the Chassis.

D 651/2: The Panzerkampfwagen II (2 cm) Sd. Kfz. 121) Variant A Chassis No.20001 to 23000 Part 2: Spare parts list.

D 653/1: Panzerkampfwagen IV (Sd. Kfz. 161). Variant A to F. Device Description and Operating Instructions for the Chassis.

D 653/9: The Panzerkampfwagen IV (7.5 cm) (VsKfz. 622) Variant A to D Chassis no. 80000 to 80750 loading plan, 10.1.1939.

---

[199] BArch, RH/8/5909: Verzeichnis der geheimen außerplanmäßigen Heeres-Vorschriften (D+), März 1937 / Januar 1938, S. 16.

[200] BArch, RH 1/384: H. Dv. 1/8 Kriegssoll (Heer) an Vorschriften – Heft 8 – Panzertruppe-Feldheer, Oktober 1943.

Ergänzung 2: Glossar

Abteilung / Bataillon: Beim deutschen Heer wurden Einheiten in der Stärke eines Bataillons, die Teil einer bestimmten Truppengattung waren (wie zum Beispiel Panzer, Artillerie oder Nachrichtentruppe) als „Abteilungen" nicht „Bataillone" bezeichnet. „Bataillon" wurde in erster Linie bei „infanterielastigen" Einheiten wie Infanterie-, Pionier- und Maschinengewehrbataillone genutzt[201].

Eine Panzerabteilung bestand im Sommer 1941 aus zwei leichten und einer mittleren Kompanie, diesen umfassten insgesamt ca. 70 Panzer. Ein Infanteriebataillon umfasste ca. 860 Mann.

Anschluß / Anschlußmann: Der Anschluß / Anschlußmann war bei der Infanterie üblicherweise ein Schütze, eine Gruppe oder Zug, welcher als Referenz für Abstände und Zwischenräume genommen wurde: „Der Anschluß soll bis zum Eintritt in den Infanteriekampf die Bewegungen der Truppenteile in Einklang bringen und den Zusammenhang sicherstellen. Im Kampf hat stets der am weitesten Vorgedrungene den Anschluß"[202]. Dementsprechend ist anzunehmen, dass der Anschluß in diesem Kontext ein Panzer oder eine Panzer Einheit ist[203].

Division: Eine Panzerdivision hatte im Sommer 1941 zwei bis drei Panzerabteilungen mit insgesamt 147 – 299 Panzern[204]. Eine Infanterie-Division umfasste etwa 17 000 Mann.

Durchbruch: Der Durchbruch ist die Fortführung des Einbruchs. Ziel ist es, den Zusammenhang der feindlichen Front zu brechen. Hierbei ist es wichtig bei der Durchbruchsstelle die jeweiligen Frontenden zu umfassen[205].

---

[201] Siehe zum Beispiel: Gesterding, Schwatlo; Feyerabend, ohne Vorname: Unteroffizierthemen. Fünfte, neubearbeite Auflage. E. S. Mittler & Sohn: Berlin, 1938, S. 21; Buchner, Alex: Das Handbuch der deutschen Infanterie 1939-1945. Podzun-Pallas: Friedberg, 1987, S. 4.

[202] Kühlwein, Fritz: Die Gruppe im Gefecht. (Die neue Gruppe). E. S. Mittler & Sohn: Berlin, 1940, S. 7.

[203] Kühlwein, Fritz: Die Gruppe im Gefecht. (Die neue Gruppe). E. S. Mittler & Sohn: Berlin, 1940, S. 7 sowie H. Dv. 130/2a: Ausbildungsvorschrift für die Infanterie. Heft 2a: Die Schützenkompanie. Verlag „Offene Worte", Berlin, 16. März 1941, S. 109.

[204] Mueller-Hillebrand, Burkhart: Das deutsche Heer 1933-1945. Band II. E. S. Mittler & Sohn: Frankfurt am Main, 1956, S. 107.

[205] Kühlwein, Fritz: Die Gruppe im Gefecht. (Die neue Gruppe). E. S. Mittler & Sohn: Berlin, 1940, S. 8.

Supplement 2: Glossary (sorted as per the German Version)

Battalion (Abteilung / Batallion): In the German army, units of some arms (like tanks, artillery, signal, etc.) with the strength of a battalion were called "Abteilung" not "Batallion". "Batallion" was only used for units like "infantry-heavy" units like infantry, engineers and machine-gun battalions[206].

A tank battalion in summer 1941 consisted of two light and one medium company amounting to an approximate total of 70 tanks. One infantry battalion consisted of about 860 men.

Contact / Connecting File (Anschluß / Anschlußmann): The contact / connecting file in infantry units was usually a riflemen, squad or platoon, which functioned as a reference for distance and spaces: "The contact shall bring the movements of the units into harmony until the start of the infantry combat and ensure the cohesion. During combat the most advanced always has the contact"[207]. Hence it can be assumed that the contact in this context was a tank or tank unit[208].

Division (Division): In summer 1941 a tank division had two to three tank battalions with a total of 147 - 299 tanks[209]. An infantry division consisted of about 17 000 men.

Penetration (Durchbruch): The penetration is the continuation of the break-in (*Einbruch*). The objective is to break the cohesion of the enemy front. Thereby it is important to encircle the respective front sections at the penetration point[210].

---

[206] Example: Gesterding, Schwatlo; Feyerabend: Unteroffizierthemen. Fünfte, neubearbeite Auflage. E. S. Mittler & Sohn: Berlin, 1938, S. 21; Buchner, Alex: Das Handbuch der deutschen Infanterie 1939-1945. Podzun-Pallas: Friedberg, 1987, S. 4.

[207] Kühlwein, Fritz: Die Gruppe im Gefecht. (Die neue Gruppe). E. S. Mittler & Sohn: Berlin, 1940, S. 7.

[208] Kühlwein, Fritz: Die Gruppe im Gefecht. (Die neue Gruppe). E. S. Mittler & Sohn: Berlin, 1940, S. 7 sowie H. Dv. 130/2a: Ausbildungsvorschrift für die Infanterie. Heft 2a: Die Schützenkompanie. Verlag "Offene Worte", Berlin, 16. März 1941, S. 109.

[209] Mueller-Hillebrand, Burkhart: Das Deutsche Heer 1933-1945. Volume II. E. S. Mittler & Son: Frankfurt am Main, 1956, S. 107.

[210] Kühlwein, Fritz: Die Gruppe im Gefecht. (Die neue Gruppe). E. S. Mittler & Sohn: Berlin, 1940, S. 8.

Einbruch: Der Einbruch ist das Ergebnis eines gelungenen Angriffs, der in die vorderste Stellung des Feindes eingedrungen ist[211].

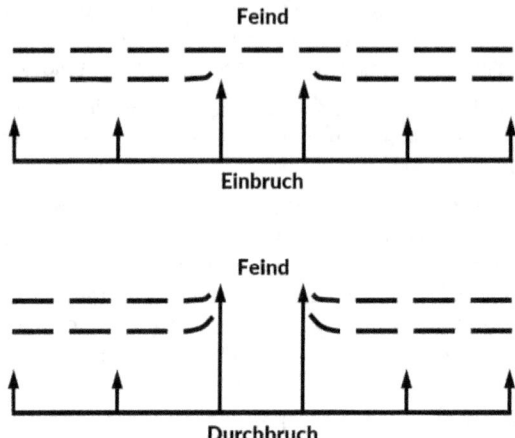

Einsatz, geschlossen: Der Begriff „geschlossener Einsatz" kommt häufig in deutschen Vorschriften des Zweiten Weltkrieges vor. Eine Einheit geschlossen einzusetzen, bedeutet ihre taktische Elemente gemeinsam einzusetzen, siehe folgende Beispiele für Infanterie (1944) und Panzer (1941 und 1943):

„In der Regel ist der M.P.-Zug geschlossen einzusetzen. Der Einsatz der einzelnen M.P.-Gruppen bildet die Ausnahme."[212]

„Die mittlere Panzerkompanie bildet mit ihren 14 Kampfwagenkanonen (7,5 cm) das Rückgrat der Panzerabteilung. Diese starke Feuerkraft gilt es – im allgemeinen durch geschlossenen Einsatz – schnell an entscheidender Stelle zu vernichtender Wirkung zu bringen."[213]

---

[211] Kühlwein, Fritz: Die Gruppe im Gefecht. (Die neue Gruppe). E. S. Mittler & Sohn: Berlin, 1940, S. 8.

[212] BArch, RH 11-I/83: Merkblatt 25a/16: Vorläufiges Merkblatt „Der M.P.-Zug der Grenadier-Kompanie", 1.2.1944, S. 15.

[213] H.Dv. 470/7: Ausbildungsvorschrift für die Panzertruppe. Heft 7: Die mittlere Panzerkompanie. Reichsdruckerei, Berlin, Germany, 1. Mai 1941, S. 5.

Break-in (Einbruch): The break-in is the result of a successful attack that breached into the enemy's foremost lines[214].

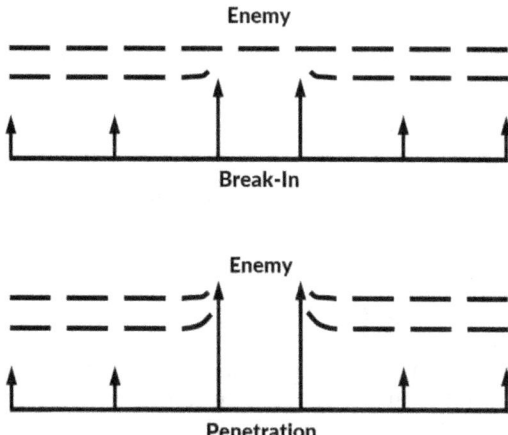

Employment of the Whole Unit (Einsatz, geschlossen): The term "geschlossener Einsatz"[215] is often used in German regulations of the Second World War. To employ a unit as "geschlossen", means to employ its tactical elements together, see the following examples for infantry (1944) and tanks (1941 and 1943):

"As a rule, the SMG[216]-platoon should be used as a whole. The use of the individual SMG-squads is the exception."[217]

"The medium tank company with its 14 vehicle-mounted guns (7.5 cm) forms the backbone of the tank battalion[218]. This strong firepower must be brought - in general by employing the unit as a whole - quickly to a decisive point and applied for destructive effect."[219]

---

[214] Kühlwein, Fritz: Die Gruppe im Gefecht. (Die neue Gruppe). E. S. Mittler & Sohn: Berlin, 1940, S. 8.

[215] The literal translation of "geschlossener Einsatz" would be "closed employment".

[216] Technically, this was not a submachine gun.

[217] BArch, RH 11-I/83: Merkblatt 25a/16: Vorläufiges Merkblatt „Der M.P.-Zug der Grenadier-Kompanie", 1.2.1944, S. 15.

[218] In the German Army, units of some arms (like tanks, artillery, etc.) with the strength of a battalion, were called "Abteilung" (literally detachment/department) not "Battalions".

[219] H.Dv. 470/7: Ausbildungsvorschrift für die Panzertruppe. Heft 7: Die mittlere Panzerkompanie. Reichsdruckerei, Berlin, Germany, 1. Mai 1941, S. 5.

„Der geschlossene Einsatz [im Wald und im Gebirge] der Kompanie bildet die Ausnahme. In der Regel werden Halbzüge oder einzelne Wagen die angreifenden Schützen beim Vorgehen unterstützen."[220]

„In der Verteidigung halte die Wagen gedeckt und mindestens zugweise geschlossen zusammen, damit sie vom Fahrer und Bordschützen besetzt, wirksam zum Gegenstoss [sic!] antreten können."[221]

Aber auch in Befehlen vom Oberkommandos der Wehrmacht (OKW) wurde dieser Begriff verwendet:

„Für den diesen Einsatz gelten dabei folgende Richtlinien:

a) Die Luftwaffen-Feldbrigaden sind geschlossen einzusetzen. Ein Zerreißen der Verbände hat zu unterbleiben."[222]

Ein Problem ist jedoch, dass es wir noch keine passende englische Übersetzung für „geschlossener Einsatz" gefunden haben. In unserer Übersetzung der *H.Dv. 470/7* hatten wir uns nach langem hin und her für „combined employment" entschieden. Dies halten wir inzwischen für falsch, da „combined" die Kombination von mehreren verschiedenen Elementen impliziert. Wir haben uns mit mehreren Personen zu dem Thema ausgetauscht, so schlug zum Beispiel Dr. Leo Niehorster „massed employment" vor.[223] Dies würde auch mit dem *Field Manual 17-32: The Tank Company, Light and Medium* vom August 1942 einhergehen, wo es bezüglich dem Einsatz im Dschungel heißt:

„In general, because of their sensitiveness to terrain, tanks are unsuited for mass employment in jungles."[224]

Allerdings ist hier das Problem ist, dass es auch den „massierten Einsatz" – wenn auch seltener – in deutschen Vorschriften gab und hier handelte es sich um den konzentrierten Einsatz von Truppen an einer gewissen Stelle.

---

[220] H.Dv. 470/7: Die mittlere Panzerkompanie, S. 68.
[221] TsAMO, F 500, Op. 12480, D 137: Nachrichtenblatt der Panzertruppen. Nr. 1, 15. Juli 1943, S. 10.
[222] Schramm, Percy E. (Hrsg.): Kriegstagebuch des OKW. Eine Dokumentation: 1942. Band 4. Teilband 2. Bechtermünz: Augsburg, Germany, 2005, S. 1299. Anlage 24: Führerbefehl vom 13. September 1942 betr. Ablösung abgekämpfter Divisionen aus dem Osten.
[223] Email Leo Niehorster vom 28. Juli 2020.
[224] FM 17-32: Armored Force Field Manual: The Tank Company, Light and Medium. War Department: Washington, USA, August, 1942, p. 77.

"The employment as a whole company [in forests and mountains] is the exception. As a rule, half-platoons or individual vehicles will support the attacking riflemen."[225]

"In the defense, keep the vehicles covered and together at minimum at a platoon strength, so that they, manned by the driver and gunner, can effectively take up the hasty counterattack[226]."[227]

But this term was also used in orders from the High Command of the Wehrmacht (OKW):

"The following guidelines apply for the employment:

a) The Luftwaffe-field brigades are to be employed as a whole. The units must not be torn apart."[228]

One problem is that we have not yet found a suitable English translation for "geschlossener Einsatz". In our translation of the *H.Dv. 470/7* we had decided after a long back and forth for "combined employment". We now think that this is wrong, because "combined" implies the combination of several different elements. We exchanged views with several people on the subject, for example Dr. Leo Niehorster suggested "massed employment".[229] This would also be in line with *Field Manual 17-32: The Tank Company, Light and Medium* of August 1942, which states with regard to the use in the jungle:

"In general, because of their sensitiveness to terrain, tanks are unsuited for mass employment in jungles."[230]

However, this created another problem because "massive employment" is also used - albeit less frequently - in German regulations, pointing to the concentrated employment of troops at a certain point.

---

[225] H.Dv. 470/7: Die mittlere Panzerkompanie, S. 68.

[226] The Germans distinguished between a hasty counterattack ("Gegenstoß") and regular counterattack ("Gegenangriff"). See Glossary: Hasty Counterattack (Gegenstoß).

[227] TsAMO, F 500, Op. 12480, D 137: Nachrichtenblatt der Panzertruppen. Nr. 1, 15. Juli 1943, S. 10.

[228] Schramm, Percy E. (Hrsg.): Kriegstagebuch des OKW. Eine Dokumentation: 1942. Band 4. Teilband 2. Bechtermünz: Augsburg, Germany, 2005, S. 1299. Anlage 24: Führerbefehl vom 13. September 1942 betr. Ablösung abgekämpfter Divisionen aus dem Osten.

[229] Email Leo Niehorster from 28. July 2020.

[230] FM 17-32: Armored Force Field Manual: The Tank Company, Light and Medium. War Department: Washington, USA, August, 1942, p. 77.

Im Englischen finden sich eher „Negativ-Definitionen" wie zum Beispiel:

„They [larger units of the Armored Force] are to be employed on decisive missions. They must not be frittered away."[231]

„Tank attacks will be costly or will result in failure to reach their objective unless employed in decisive numbers."[232]

„The piecemeal employment of tank units is wrong; they must be used in large numbers in a coordinated effort."[233]

Sonstige Alternativen, die wir angedacht haben waren:

- Unified Employment: Das Problem hierbei ist, dass eine Einheit schon „vereinigt" ist.
- Cohesive Employment: Ähnliches Problem wie bei „unified employment".
- Closed Employment: Dies könnte leicht mit „close order" (geschlossene Ordnung) verwechselt werden und ist auch wenig aussagekräftig.
- Non-piecemeal Employment: Ist eine „Negativ-Definition".

Basierend darauf haben wir uns entschieden „geschlossener Einsatz" mit „employment of the whole unit" bzw. „employing the unit as a whole" zu übersetzen, was auch nicht einer gewissen Ironie entbehrt.

Entfaltung: Die Entfaltung dient dazu die Gefechtsbereitschaft zu erhöhen. Dementsprechend findet sie statt, wenn damit gerechnet werden muss, dass es zu einem Zusammenstoß mit dem Feind kommt. Die Entfaltung ist die Umgliederung von der Marschkolonne in mehrere Kolonnen, die eine breitere Front bilden. Dementsprechend führt die Entfaltung zu einer Verlangsamung der entfaltenden Einheiten. Ebenso wird die für den Kampf nötige Tiefengliederung vorbereitet. Der Entfaltung folgt die Entwicklung[234].

---

[231] FM 17-10: Armored Force Field Manual: Tactics and Technique. War Department: Washington, USA, March, 1942, p. 3.
[232] FM 17-10: Armored Force Field Manual: Tactics and Technique. War Department: Washington, USA, March, 1942, p. 90.
[233] FM 17-10: Armored Force Field Manual: Tactics and Technique. War Department: Washington, USA, March, 1942, p. 131.
[234] Kühlwein, Fritz: Die Gruppe im Gefecht. (Die neue Gruppe). E. S. Mittler & Sohn: Berlin, 1940, S. 8; sowie H. Dv. 300/1: Truppenführung I. Teil. E. S. Mittler & Sohn: Berlin, 1936 (1933), S. 95-96.

In English "negative definitions" are common, for example:

"They [larger units of the Armored Force] are to be employed on decisive missions. They must not be frittered away."[235]

"Tank attacks will be costly or will result in failure to reach their objective unless employed in decisive numbers."[236]

"The piecemeal employment of tank units is wrong; they must be used in large numbers in a coordinated effort."[237]

Other alternatives that we have considered were:

- Unified Employment: The problem here is that a unit is already "unified".
- Cohesive Employment: Similar problem as with "unified employment".
- Closed Employment: This could easily be confused with "close order" (geschlossene Ordnung) and is not very descriptive.
- Non-piecemeal Employment: Is a "negative-definition".

Based on this, we have decided to translate "geschlossener Einsatz" with "employment of the whole unit" or "employing the unit as a whole", which is not without a certain irony.

Preliminary deployment – "development" according to TM 30-506 (Entfaltung): Preliminary deployment serves to increase the combat readiness. Thus, it takes place, if an encounter with the enemy is likely. Preliminary deployment is the regrouping of the marching column into several columns offering a wider front. Accordingly, the preliminary deployment slows down the movement of the corresponding units. Additionally, the necessary distribution in depth required for combat is prepared. The preliminary deployment precedes the full deployment (*Entwicklung*)[238].

---

[235] FM 17-10: Armored Force Field Manual: Tactics and Technique. War Department: Washington, USA, March, 1942, p. 3.
[236] FM 17-10: Armored Force Field Manual: Tactics and Technique. War Department: Washington, USA, March, 1942, p. 90.
[237] FM 17-10: Armored Force Field Manual: Tactics and Technique. War Department: Washington, USA, March, 1942, p. 131.
[238] Kühlwein, Fritz: Die Gruppe im Gefecht. (Die neue Gruppe). E. S. Mittler & Sohn: Berlin, 1940, S. 8.

Feuerüberfall: „Schlagartiger Einsatz einer mehr oder minder großen Zahl für einen bestimmten Kampfzweck zusammengefaßter Waffen. Er ist bei allen Kampflagen anzustreben und verspricht besonderen Erfolg gegen lohnende, kurze sichtbare Ziele oder zur Einleitung einer Überraschung, z. B. beim Angriff."[239]

Entwicklung: Die Entwicklung folgt üblicherweise auf die Entfaltung. Dabei werden die Einheiten weiter aufgegliedert, um sich für den Kampf vorzubereiten. Die Entwicklung kann auch direkt aus der Marschkolonne heraus erfolgen, wenn keine Zeit zur Entfaltung ist[240].

Gefechtstroß: Der Gefechtstroß setzte sich aus geländegängigen Transportfahrzeugen, Feldküche und Handpferden – hierbei handelt es sich um Pferde, die mit der Hand gehalten werden - zusammen. Die Transportfahrzeuge führten das Material, das die Truppe auf dem Gefechtsfeld brauchte, mit sich: Munition, Betriebsstoff, Kampfmittel aller Art, Ersatzteile, Werkzeuge für kleinere Instandsetzungen, Sanitäts- und Veterinärgerät[241].

Gepäcktroß: Beim Gepäcktroß befand sich all das Gepäck, welches die kämpfende Truppe nicht unbedingt zum Marsch und Gefecht benötigte. Dementsprechend sollte sich etwa 75 % des Gepäcks der Truppe beim Gepäcktroß befinden und ca. 25 % sollte als Marschgepäck direkt am Mann sein. Typisch für den Gepäcktroß waren zusätzliche Kleidung und Vorräte für die Truppe[242].

---

[239] Haas, Walter: Soldatenlexikon. Ein Merkbuch für den Infanteriedienst. Franckh'sche Verlagshandlung: Stuttgart, Germany, o.J., S. 57.
[240] Kühlwein, Fritz: Die Gruppe im Gefecht. (Die neue Gruppe). E. S. Mittler & Sohn: Berlin, 1940, S. 8.
[241] Bieringer: Nachschubfibel. Zweite verbesserte Auflage. Verlag „Offene Worte", Berlin, 1938, S. 20.
[242] Bieringer: Nachschubfibel. Zweite verbesserte Auflage. Verlag „Offene Worte", Berlin, 1938, S. 23.

Surprise Fire (Feuerüberfall): "Abrupt employment of a more or less large number of weapons combined for a specific combat purpose. It is to be aimed at in all combat situations and promises special success against worthwhile, short visible targets or to initiate a surprise, e.g. when attacking."[243]

Full deployment – "deployment" according to TM 30-506 (Entwicklung): The full deployment usually follows the preliminary deployment (*Entfaltung*). The units are further spread out to prepare for battle. Full deployment can also take place directly from the marching column, if there is no time for a preliminary deployment[244].

Combat trains (Gefechtstroß): The combat trains were composed of cross-country capable transport vehicles, field kitchen and near horses – these are horses that are hold with the hand. The transport vehicles carried everything that was needed by the troops on the battlefield: ammunition, fuel, ordnance of all kinds, spare parts, tools for smaller maintenance, medical and veterinary equipment[245].

Baggage trains (Gepäcktroß): The baggage trains transported all the baggage, which was not necessarily needed by the men during march and engagements. Accordingly, about 75 % of the baggage should be carried by the baggage train, whereas about 25 % should be as field pack with the troops. Typical for the baggage trains were additional clothes and supplies for the troops[246].

---

[243] Haas, Walter: Soldatenlexikon. Ein Merkbuch für den Infanteriedienst. Franckh'sche Verlagshandlung: Stuttgart, Germany, o.J., S. 57.

[244] Kühlwein, Fritz: Die Gruppe im Gefecht. (Die neue Gruppe). E. S. Mittler & Sohn: Berlin, 1940, S. 8.

[245] Bieringer: Nachschubfibel. Zweite verbesserte Auflage. Verlag "Offene Worte", Berlin, 1938, S. 20.

[246] Bieringer: Nachschubfibel. Zweite verbesserte Auflage. Verlag "Offene Worte", Berlin, 1938, S. 23.

Gruppe - Panzertruppe: Eine Gruppe besteht aus 2 Panzern und ist Teil eines leichten Zuges von 5 Panzern, der aus 2 Gruppen und einem Panzer für den Zugführer besteht[247]. Dagegen besteht ein mittlerer Zug von 4 Panzern aus 2 Halbzügen zu je 2 Panzer[248].

Halbzug - Panzertruppe: Ein mittlerer Zug von 4 Panzern gliedert sich in 2 Halbzüge zu je 2 Panzern. Siehe auch Gruppe.

Hauptfeldwebel: Oft auch „Spieß" oder „Mutter der Kompanie" genannt. Hauptfeldwebel war jedoch kein militärischer Rang an sich, sondern ein Dienstposten. Das Aufgabengebiet des Hauptfeldwebels war der rückwärtige Bereich. Er kümmerte sich vor allem, um die Versorgung, wie Arbeit der Trosse, Schreibdienste etc. Er war verantwortlich für alle Aufgaben, die nicht direkt mit dem Kampf zu tun hatten[249].

Heer: Das Heer war eine der drei Teilstreitkräfte der Wehrmacht, die anderen beiden waren die Luftwaffe und Kriegsmarine. Oft wird das Heer mit der Wehrmacht verwechselt.

Kompanie: Militärische Einheit; 1941 umfasste eine mittlere Panzerkompanie 19 Panzer[250]. Eine leichte Kompanie umfasste 22 Panzer. Eine Infanteriekompanie hatte eine Stärke von ca. 200 Mann. Bei der Artillerie hieß eine Einheit in Kompanie-Stärke Batterie.

Kurskreisel: Ein Kurskreisel ist ein Gyroskop, welches die Richtung für den Fahrer angibt.

Panzerschütze: Der Panzerschütze ist nicht mit dem Richtschützen zu verwechseln! Panzerschütze war ein Rang, und zwar der niedrigste Rang in der Panzertruppe[251]. In der Wehrmacht wurden die Ränge der jeweiligen Waffengattung angepasst, z.B. war der niedrigste Rang bei der Infanterie der Schütze, bei der Artillerie der Kanonier.

---

[247] Siehe Ziffer 39.

[248] Siehe Ziffer 40.

[249] Buchner, Alex: Das Handbuch der deutschen Infanterie 1939-1945. Podzun-Pallas: Friedberg, 1987. S. 18-19.

[250] Siehe Anhang 2.

[251] Übersichtstabelle: Gesterding, Schwatlo; Feyerabend: Unteroffizierthemen. Fünfte, neubearbeite Auflage. E. S. Mittler & Sohn: Berlin, 1938, S. 36-37.

Section – Armored Troops (Gruppe - Panzertruppe): A section consists of 2 tanks and is part of a light platoon of 5 tanks, which consists of 2 sections and one tank of the platoon leader[252]. In contrast, a medium platoon consists of 4 tanks of 2 half-platoons with 2 tanks each[253].

Half-platoon (Halbzug): A platoon is divided into 2 half-platoons with 2 tanks each. See also Section.

Company sergeant major (Hauptfeldwebel): In the Wehrmacht, the company sergeant major, often referred to as "Spieß" (literally "skewer") or "mother of the company", was not a rank but an appointment. The sergeant major's area of responsibility was the rear of the company. He mainly took care of the supply, such as work of the supply train, secretarial services a of all those tasks that were not directly related to combat[254].

German Army (Heer): The German Army was one of the three branches of the Wehrmacht, the other two were the Luftwaffe and Kriegsmarine. The German Army (Heer) is often confused with the Wehrmacht.

Company (Kompanie): Military unit. A medium tank company in 1941 consisted of 19 tanks[255]. A light company in 1941 consisted of 22 tanks. One infantry company consisted of about 200 men. In artillery, one unit was called Company Strength Battery.

Course gyroscope (Kurskreisel): A course gyroscope is a gyroscope indicating direction for the driver[256].

Tank rifleman (Panzerschütze): "Panzerschütze" literally means "tank rifleman". In German it can be confused with the "gunner", who was called "Richtschütze". Yet, the "Panzerschütze" was not a role, but a rank, namely the lowest in the Armored Troops[257]. The Wehrmacht had rank names that were dependent on the branch, e.g., the lowest infantry man was a "Schütze" (rifleman), whereas the lowest artillery man was a "Kanonier" (cannoneer).

---

[252] See Number 39.

[253] See Number 40.

[254] Buchner, Alex: Das Handbuch der deutschen Infanterie 1939-1945. Podzun-Pallas: Friedberg, 1987. S. 18-19.

[255] See Appendix 2.

[256] This seems rather obvious but relates to the antiquated term "Kurskreisel" which is no longer common knowledge in Germany.

[257] For a table of various ranks see: Gesterding, Schwatlo; Feyerabend: Unteroffizierthemen. Fünfte, neubearbeite Auflage. E. S. Mittler & Sohn: Berlin, 1938, S. 36-37.

Regiment: Ein Panzerregiment war im Sommer 1941 der Kern einer Panzerdivision und umfasste zwei bis drei Panzerabteilungen, es hatte dieselbe Stärke wie eine Division abzüglich der Panzer im Stab der Panzerbrigade (8 Panzer bei der 4. Panzerdivision Sommer 1941[258]). Ein Infanterieregiment hatte um die 3000 Mann.

Schirrmeister: Kraftfahrzeug-Meister des Fuhrparks der Einheit. Hierbei handelt es sich um einen alten Namen, wobei das „Schirr" auf das Pferdegeschirr verweist.

Sonderkraftfahrzeug: Kraftfahrzeuge, die für militärische Zwecke gebaut wurden.

Stoßlinie: Die Stoßlinie war eine Referenzlinie auf Karten, die es den Einheiten erlaubte, im Gefecht darauf zu verweisen. Dies ermöglichte eine einfache Orientierung und verhinderte, dass der Feind beim Abfangen der Funksprüche die Position zurückverfolgen konnte.

Zug: Der mittlere Zug umfasste 1941 vier Panzer, der leichte Zug fünf Panzer. Ein Infanteriezug umfasste rund 50 Mann.

---

[258] Keilig, Wolf: Das deutsche Heer 1939-1945. Podzun-Verlag: Bad Nauheim: ohne Jahr, Nummer 103 / II / 18, Fußnote 2.

Regiment (Regiment): A tank regiment was the core of a tank division in summer 1941 and contained two to three tank divisions, it had the same strength as a division minus the tanks in the staff of the tank brigade (8 tanks at the 4th tank division summer 1941[259]). An infantry regiment had about 3 000 men.

Maintenance Technical Sergeant (Schirrmeister): Foreman of the unit's vehicle inventory. The German original "Schirrmeister" literally translated means "Horse tackle master", which is a constructed from the words "Pferdegeschirr", a horse harness or tackle and "Meister", master.

Special Motor Vehicle (Sonderkraftfahrzeug): Motor vehicles built for military purposes.

Axis reference line (Stoßlinie): The axis reference line was a reference line on maps that allowed units to use it for communicating their relative position in an engagement. This allowed for quick orientation and coordination, while it prevented the enemy from locating the units when intercepting the radio messages.

Platoon (Zug): In 1941 the medium platoon consisted of four tanks, the light platoon five tanks. One infantry platoon contained about 50 men.

---

[259] Keilig, Wolf: Das deutsche Heer 1939-1945. Podzun-Verlag: Bad Nauheim: ohne Jahr, Nummer 103 / II / 18, Fußnote 2.

Eine Anmerkung zur Benutzung von „Deployment" im Bezug auf „Entfaltung" und „Entwicklung"

Eine Kernreferenz in unserer Arbeit war selbstverständlich das US Army Technical Manual TM 30-506 German Military Dictionary vom Mai 1944. Es enthielt die folgende Passage:

„Thus, although the literal translation of Entwicklung would be 'development,' a study of the German operations manual reveals that Entwicklung follows Entfaltung ('development') and hence is the equivalent of 'deployment.' Translations have been provided (generally with a note of explanation) only where equivalents do not exist or could not be found."[260]

Auch in zeitgenössischen US Field Manuals wurde „development" verwendet[261]. Hier gibt es allerdings ein Problem mit der heutigen Terminologie, z. B.: hat sich die Terminologie in der US Armee geändert wie uns Major Nicholas Moran mitteilte. „Developing" ist eine andere Handlung und passiert nun in einer späteren Phase[262].

Zusätzlich haben wir auch Bruce Condells und David T. Zabeckis Übersetzung der H. Dv. 300 Truppenführung benutzt, sie nutzen die folgende Übersetzung:

„Preliminary deployment, *Entfaltung*, followed by *Entwicklung*, full deployment."[263] (Kursiv wie im Original.)

Außerdem ist es wichtig festzustellen, dass im deutschen Heer die „Entfaltung" eine größere Bedeutung als die „Entwicklung" hatte, dies ist aus der Stellungnahme im TM 30-506 nicht ersichtlich. Allerdings enthalten die deutschen Heeresdruckvorschriften üblicherweise „Entfaltung" im Inhaltsverzeichnis, z. B.: H. Dv. 470/6: Die leichte Panzerkompanie oder H. Dv. 130/2a: Die Schützenkompanie. Auch die wichtige Richtlinie H. Dv. 300/1: Truppenführung I. Teil enthält „Entfaltung" im Register. Zum Vergleich, „Entwicklung" ist weder im Inhaltsverzeichnis noch im Register dieser Publikationen enthalten.

Deshalb nutzen wir den Ansatz von Condell und Zabecki mit „preliminary deployment" für „Entfaltung" und „full deployment" für „Entwicklung".

---

[260] TM 30-506 German Military Dictionary, 1944, p. iii.

[261] In Referenz zu FM 7-5 Organization and Tactics of Infantry: The Rifle Battalions, 1940, p. 261. FM 17-10: Armored Force Field Manual: Tactics and Technique, 1942, p. 241.

[262] Siehe FM 17-15: Tank Platoon. Headquarters of the Army, USA, April, 1996, p. 65, siehe Abschnitt "Evaluate/Develop the Situation".

[263] Condell, Bruce (ed.); Zabecki, David T. (ed.): On the German Art of War. Truppenführung. Stackpole Books: Mechanicsburg, PA, USA, 2009 (2001), p. 51.

A Note about the Use of "Deployment" in Regards to "Entfaltung" and "Entwicklung"

One key reference for our work was of course the US Army Technical Manual TM 30-506 German Military Dictionary from May 1944. And it contained the following passage:

"Thus, although the literal translation of Entwicklung would be 'development,' a study of the German operations manual reveals that Entwicklung follows Entfaltung ('development') and hence is the equivalent of 'deployment.' Translations have been provided (generally with a note of explanation) only where equivalents do not exist or could not be found."[264]

In contemporary US Field Manuals "development" was also used[265]. Yet, the main problem with this terminology is that nowadays, e.g., in the US Army the terminology has changed as pointed out to us by Major Nicholas Moran. "Developing" is a different action nowadays and happens at a later stage[266].

Additionally, we also looked at Bruce Condell's and David T. Zabecki's translation of the H. Dv. 300 Unit Command, they used the following translation:

"Preliminary deployment, *Entfaltung*, followed by *Entwicklung*, full deployment."[267] (*Italics* as in the original.)

Furthermore, it is important that in the German Army, "Entfaltung" had more significance than "Entwicklung", this is not apparent from the TM 30-506 statement. German Army Regulations tend to include "Entfaltung" in their table of contents, e.g., H. Dv. 470/6: The Light Tank Company or H. Dv. 130/2a: The Rifle Company. Similarly, the crucial guideline H. Dv. 300/1: Unit Command Volume I contains "Entfaltung" in its index. In contrast "Entwicklung" is not mentioned in the table of contents nor the index of these publications.

As such we use the approach from Condell and Zabecki with "preliminary deployment" for "Entfaltung" and "full deployment" for "Entwicklung".

---

[264] TM 30-506 German Military Dictionary, 1944, p. iii.

[265] In Reference to FM 7-5 Organization and Tactics of Infantry: The Rifle Battalions, 1940, p. 261. FM 17-10: Armored Force Field Manual: Tactics and Technique, 1942, p. 241.

[266] See FM 17-15: Tank Platoon. Headquarters of the Army, USA, April, 1996, p. 65, see Section "Evaluate/Develop the Situation".

[267] Condell, Bruce (ed.); Zabecki, David T. (ed.): On the German Art of War. Truppenführung. Stackpole Books: Mechanicsburg, PA, USA, 2009 (2001), p. 51.

Ergänzung 3: Visualisierung zu Anlage 2 Stärkenachweisung mittlere Panzerkompanie

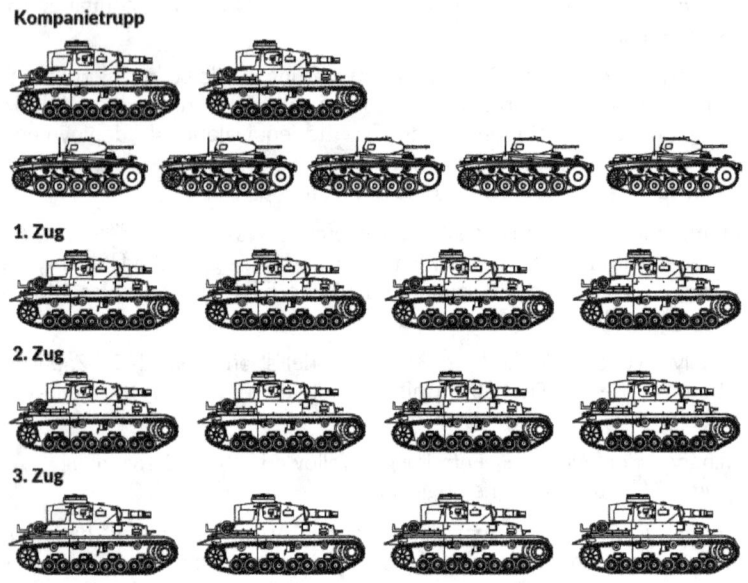

Hierbei handelt es sich um die Gliederung laut der Vorschrift, allerdings war für die Operation Barbarossa der 3. Zug nicht genehmigt.[268]

---

[268] Niehorster, Leo W.G., German World War II Organizational Series. Volume 3/I: Mechanized Army Divisions and Waffen-SS Units (22 June 1941), Milton Keynes, 2007, p. 34.

Supplement 3: Visualization of Appendix 2 Strength of Medium Tank Company

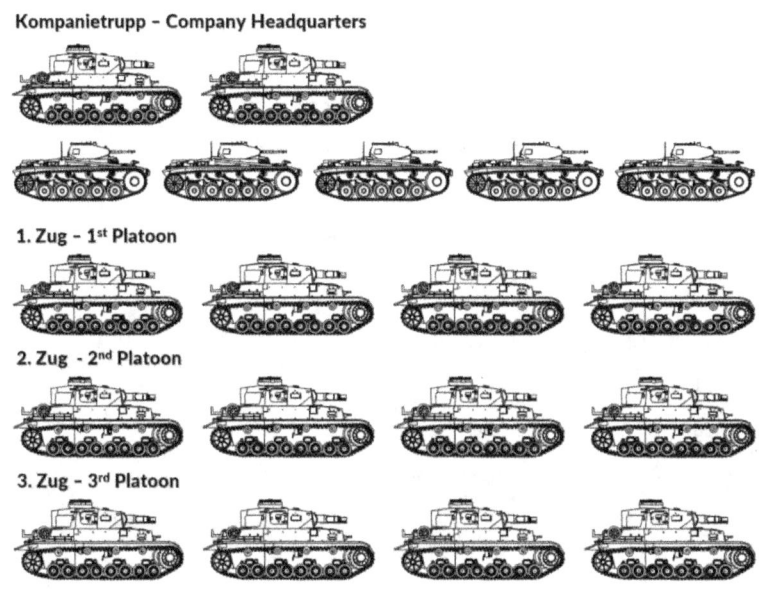

This is the outline according to the regulation, however, for Operation Barbarossa the 3rd Platoon was not authorized.[269]

---

[269] Niehorster, Leo W.G., German World War II Organizational Series. Volume 3/I: Mechanized Army Divisions and Waffen-SS Units (22 June 1941), Milton Keynes, 2007, p. 34.

Ergänzung 4: Ränge – Deutsches Reich, USA & UdSSR

Offiziere[270]

Deutsches Heer	US Army	Rote Armee
-	-	Generalissimus
Generalfeldmarschall	General of the Army	Marshal Sovetskogo Soyuza
Generaloberst	General	General Armiyi
General	Lieutenant General	General Polkovnik
Generalleutnant	Major General	General Leytenant
Generalmajor	Brigadier General	General Major
Oberst	Colonel	Polkovnik
Oberstleutnant	Lieutenant Colonel	Podpolkovnik
Major	Major	Major
Hauptmann	Captain	Kapetan
Oberleutnant	1st Lieutenant	Starshiy Leytenant
Leutnant	2nd Lieutenant	Mladshiy Leytenant

Mannschaften und Unteroffiziere[271]

Deutsches Heer	US Army	Rote Armee
Stabsfeldwebel	Master Sergeant[272]	-
Oberfeldwebel	Master/First Sergeant	Starshina
Feldwebel	Technical Sergeant	Starshiy Serzhant
Unterfeldwebel	Staff Sergeant	-
Unteroffizier	Sergeant	Serzhant
-	Corporal	Mladhsiy Serzhant
Hauptgefreiter	Private First Class	Yefreytor
Obergefreiter		
Gefreiter		
Obersoldat	-	-
Soldat	Private	Krasnoarmeyets

---

[270] Glantz, David et al.: Slaughterhouse: The Encyclopedia of the Eastern Front. Military Book Club: USA, 2002. p. viii. Anmerkung: Stahel, David: Operation Barbarossa and Germany's Defeat in the East. Cambridge University Press: Cambridge, UK, 2011 (2009), p. xv hat in manchen Fällen andere Angaben.

[271] Glantz, David et al.: Slaughterhouse: The Encyclopedia of the Eastern Front. Military Book Club: USA, 2002. p. viii. Anmerkung: Stahel, David: Operation Barbarossa and Germany's Defeat in the East. Cambridge University Press: Cambridge, UK, 2011 (2009), p. xv hat in manchen Fällen andere Angaben.

[272] Note that the Sergeant Major was not a rank in the US Army during the Second World War, see Glantz, David et al.: Slaughterhouse: The Encyclopedia of the Eastern Front. Military Book Club: USA, 2002. p. viii.

Supplement 4: Ranks – Germany, USA & USSR

Officers[273]

German Army	US Army	Red Army
-	-	Generalissimus
Generalfeldmarschall	General of the Army	Marshal Sovetskogo Soyuza
Generaloberst	General	General Armiyi
General	Lieutenant General	General Polkovnik
Generalleutnant	Major General	General Leytenant
Generalmajor	Brigadier General	General Major
Oberst	Colonel	Polkovnik
Oberstleutnant	Lieutenant Colonel	Podpolkovnik
Major	Major	Major
Hauptmann	Captain	Kapetan
Oberleutnant	1st Lieutenant	Starshiy Leytenant
Leutnant	2nd Lieutenant	Mladshiy Leytenant

Enlisted Men and Non-Commissioned Officers[274]

German Army	US Army	Red Army
Stabsfeldwebel	Master Sergeant[275]	-
Oberfeldwebel	Master/First Sergeant	Starshina
Feldwebel	Technical Sergeant	Starshiy Serzhant
Unterfeldwebel	Staff Sergeant	-
Unteroffizier	Sergeant	Serzhant
-	Corporal	Mladshiy Serzhant
Hauptgefreiter	Private First Class	Yefreytor
Obergefreiter		
Gefreiter		
Obersoldat	-	-
Soldat	Private	Krasnoarmeyets

---

[273] Glantz, David et al.: Slaugtherhouse: The Encyclopedia of the Eastern Front. Military Book Club: USA, 2002. p. viii. Anmerkung: Stahel, David: Operation Barbarossa and Germany's Defeat in the East. Cambridge University Press: Cambridge, UK, 2011 (2009), p. xv has in some cases different translations.

[274] Glantz, David et al.: Slaughterhouse: The Encyclopedia of the Eastern Front. Military Book Club: USA, 2002. p. viii. See also: Stahel, David: Operation Barbarossa and Germany's Defeat in the East. Cambridge University Press: Cambridge, UK, 2011 (2009), p. xv has in some cases different translations.

[275] Note that the Sergeant Major was not a rank in the US Army during the Second World War, see Glantz, David et al.: Slaughterhouse: The Encyclopedia of the Eastern Front. Military Book Club: USA, 2002. p. viii.

Ergänzung 5: Die Panzerkampfwagen I bis IV

Ein kurzer Überblick über die Panzerkampfwagen I bis IV, die für den Zeitraum dieser Druckvorschrift die relevanten Typen darstellen.

Panzerkampfwagen I

Der Panzerkampfwagen I war der erste deutsche Panzer, der nachdem 1. Weltkrieg in Serie gebaut wurde. Er wird oft als „Trainingspanzer" bezeichnet. Diese Aussage ist jedoch nur bedingt korrekt. Der Panzer war mit gehärteten Panzerplatten und 2 Maschinengewehren ausgestattet und sowohl diese Ausstattung als auch die in den taktischen Vorschriften festgelegten Einsatzgrundsätze für diese „MG-Wagen" sprechen eindeutig gegen die „Trainingspanzer"-Behauptung Guderians. In den 30er Jahren konnte es sich die Wehrmacht nicht leisten einen Panzer zu entwickeln, der nicht für den Kampfeinsatz gedacht war. Des Weiteren gab es eine Trainingspanzer-Variante des Panzer I ohne Turm und Bewaffnung.

Allerdings war der Panzer I in dem Sinne ein „Ausbildungspanzer", dass die deutschen Panzertruppen damit den Einsatz von größeren Panzerverbänden trainierte, weil zunächst nicht genügend schwerere Panzertypen vorhanden waren. Er war daher von zentraler Bedeutung für den Aufbau der Deutschen Panzerwaffe, insbesondere unter Berücksichtigung der schnellen Aufrüstung nach 1933. Der Panzer I hatte sowohl Befürworter als auch Gegner. Mehrere Generäle, die sich seiner Schwächen bewusst waren, sprachen sich gegen einen Einsatz dieses Panzers aus. Andere Generäle drängten hingegen auf die schnelle Aufrüstung der Wehrmacht[276]. Diese wurde schließlich durchgeführt. Zu Kriegsbeginn 1939 waren 36 % aller deutschen Panzer, die gegen Polen eingesetzt wurden, Panzer I[277]. Beim Frankreichfeldzug im Mai 1940 war dieser Anteil bereits auf 20 % gesunken,[278] zu Beginn der Operation Barbarossa im Sommer 1941 auf 5 %[279].

---

[276] Pöhlmann, Markus: Der Panzer und die Mechanisierung des Krieges: Eine deutsche Geschichte 1890 bis 1945. Ferdinand Schöningh: Paderborn, 2016, S. 230-243.

[277] Jentz, Thomas L.: Panzertruppen. The Complete Guide to the Creation & Combat Employment of Germany's Tank Force. 1933-1942. Schiffer Military History: Atglen, USA, 1996, p. 88.

[278] Frieser, Karl-Heinz: Blitzkrieg-Legende. Der Westfeldzug 1940. 4. Auflage. Oldenbourg Verlag: München, 2012, S. 44.

[279] Mueller-Hillebrand, Burkhart: Das deutsche Heer 1933-1945. Band II. E. S. Mittler & Sohn: Frankfurt am Main, 1956, S. 106.

Supplement 5: The Panzerkampfwagen I to IV

A brief overview of the Panzerkampfwagen I to IV, which represent the relevant types for the period of this publication.

Panzerkampfwagen I

The Panzerkampfwagen I was the first German tank to be built in series after World War 1. It is often referred to as a "training tank". However, this statement is only partially correct. The tank was equipped with hardened armor plates and 2 machine guns and this equipment – and also the tactical guidelines for these "MG-vehicles" defined in regulations clearly speak against Guderian's assertion that this was merely a "training tank". In the 1930s, the Wehrmacht could not afford to develop a tank that was not intended for combat use. Furthermore, there was a training tank variant of the Panzer I, built without a turret and armament.

Yet, the Panzer I was an "education tank" in the sense that it allowed the German tank troops to be trained and gain experience in the operation of larger tank units, since initially there were not enough heavier tank types available. It was therefore of central importance for the development of the German Armor Branch, especially considering the accelerated rearmament from 1933 onwards. This caused some controversy, as the Panzer I also had its opponents. Several generals who were aware of its weaknesses spoke out against the use of this tank. Others urged the Wehrmacht to arm itself quickly and the Panzer I was considered necessary for this very reason[280]. This reasoning eventually overcame the opposition. When Germany invaded Poland in 1939, 36% of all German tanks used during the attack were Panzer I[281]. In May 1940 during the French campaign this share had already fallen to 20%[282]; by summer 1941 for Operation Barbarossa to 5%[283].

---

[280] Pöhlmann, Markus: Der Panzer und die Mechanisierung des Krieges: Eine deutsche Geschichte 1890 bis 1945. Ferdinand Schöningh: Paderborn, 2016, S. 230-243.

[281] Jentz, Thomas L.: Panzertruppen. The Complete Guide to the Creation & Combat Employment of Germany's Tank Force. 1933-1942. Schiffer Military History: Atglen, USA, 1996, p. 88.

[282] Frieser, Karl-Heinz: Blitzkrieg-Legende. Der Westfeldzug 1940. 4. Auflage. Oldenbourg Verlag: München, 2012, S. 44.

[283] Mueller-Hillebrand, Burkhart: Das deutsche Heer 1933-1945. Band II. E. S. Mittler & Sohn: Frankfurt am Main, 1956, S. 106.

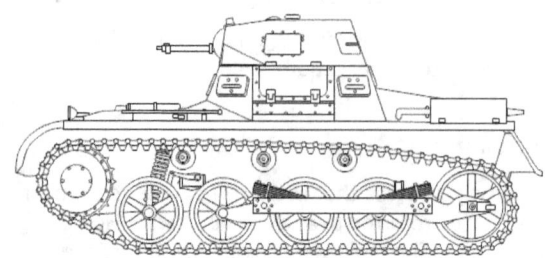

Panzerkampfwagen I Ausführung A

Technische Daten (Ausführung A)[284]

Besatzung: 2 Mann

Länge: 4,02 m

Breite: 2,06 m

Höhe: 1,72 m

Kampfgewicht: 5,4 t

Leistung: 60 PS

Höchstgeschwindigkeit: 37 km/h

Reichweite: 140 km (Straße), 93 km (Gelände)

Bewaffnung: 2 x 7,92-mm-MG 13

---

[284] Jentz, Thomas L.: Panzertruppen. The Complete Guide to the Creation & Combat Employment of Germany's Tank Force. 1933-1942. Schiffer Military History: Atglen, USA, 1996, p. 278.

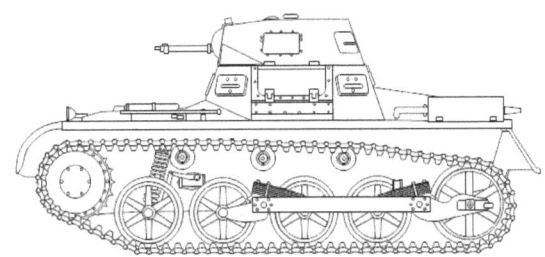

Panzerkampfwagen I Ausführung A

Technical data (Ausführung A[285])[286]

Crew: 2 men

Length: 4.02 m

Width: 2.06 m

Height: 1.72 m

Combat weight: 5.4 t

Power output: 60 hp

Maximum speed: 37 km/h

Range: 140 km (road), 93 km (terrain)

Armament: 2 x 7.92 mm MG 13

---

[285] Ausführung (shortened: Ausf.) translates to "Variant", with the following letter detailing the exact variant of the tank. In this case, "Variant A".

[286] Jentz, Thomas L.: Panzertruppen. The Complete Guide to the Creation & Combat Employment of Germany's Tank Force. 1933-1942. Schiffer Military History: Atglen, USA, 1996, p. 278.

Panzerkampfwagen II

Der Panzerkampfwagen II wurde eingeführt, da die Entwicklung der Panzer III und IV zulange dauerte. Er war somit als Zwischenlösung gedacht. Seine Bewaffnung mit einer 2 cm Maschinenkanone und einem MG war zwar besser als die des Panzer I, allerdings dem Panzer III und IV weit unterlegen. Die Entwicklung und Fertigung verlief relativ chaotisch, insbesondere weil einige Unternehmen eingebunden wurden, die bisher keine Erfahrung in der Panzerrüstung gesammelt hatten[287]. Zu Kriegsbeginn 1939 war der Panzer II der zahlenmäßig am häufigsten vertretene deutsche Panzer, mit einem Anteil von 40 % aller deutschen Panzer, die gegen Polen eingesetzt wurden[288]. Beim Frankreichfeldzug im Mai 1940 war dieser Anteil bereits auf 37 % gesunken, zahlenmäßig war der Panzer II aber noch immer der häufigste deutsche Kampfwagen[289]. Erst im Sommer 1941, während der Operation Barbarossa, war der Anteil auf 22 %. Damit stand der Panzer II quantitativ an dritter Stelle, der zweithäufigste Panzer war der Panzer 38(t) mit einem Anteil von 23 %[290].

---

[287] Pöhlmann, Markus: Der Panzer und die Mechanisierung des Krieges: Eine deutsche Geschichte 1890 bis 1945. Ferdinand Schöningh: Paderborn, 2016, S. 269.

[288] Jentz, Thomas L.: Panzertruppen. The Complete Guide to the Creation & Combat Employment of Germany's Tank Force. 1933-1942. Schiffer Military History: Atglen, USA, 1996, p. 88.

[289] Frieser, Karl-Heinz: Blitzkrieg-Legende. Der Westfeldzug 1940. 4. Auflage. Oldenbourg Verlag: München, 2012, S. 44.

[290] Mueller-Hillebrand, Burkhart: Das deutsche Heer 1933-1945. Band II. E. S. Mittler & Sohn: Frankfurt am Main, 1956, S. 106.

Panzerkampfwagen II

The Panzerkampfwagen II was introduced when the development of the Panzer III and IV took longer than expected. It was thus intended as an interim solution. Its armament consisted of a single 2 cm cannon and co-axial MG and was thus more heavily armed than the Panzer I, while remaining clearly inferior to Panzer III and IV. The development and production were relatively chaotic, especially because some companies involved had no previous experience with tank production and weaponry[291]. In September 1939, Panzer IIs represented the majority of German tanks in terms of numbers, accounting for 40% of all German tanks used against Poland[292]. In May 1940, during the French campaign, this share had fallen to only 37%, remaining the largest share in terms of numbers[293]. Only by the summer of 1941 for Operation Barbarossa had the share fallen to 22 %. Thus, relegating it to third place, this was only 1% off the second most common tank, the Panzer38(t) of Czechoslovakian origin[294].

---

[291] Pöhlmann, Markus: Der Panzer und die Mechanisierung des Krieges: Eine deutsche Geschichte 1890 bis 1945. Ferdinand Schöningh: Paderborn, 2016, S. 269.

[292] Jentz, Thomas L.: Panzertruppen. The Complete Guide to the Creation & Combat Employment of Germany's Tank Force. 1933-1942. Schiffer Military History: Atglen, USA, 1996, p. 88.

[293] Frieser, Karl-Heinz: Blitzkrieg-Legende. Der Westfeldzug 1940. 4. Auflage. Oldenbourg Verlag: München, 2012, S. 44.

[294] Mueller-Hillebrand, Burkhart: Das deutsche Heer 1933-1945. Band II. E. S. Mittler & Sohn: Frankfurt am Main, 1956, S. 106.

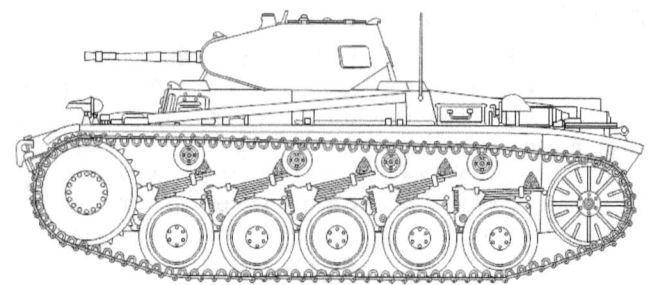

Panzerkampfwagen II Ausführung C

Technische Daten (Ausführung C)[295]

Besatzung: 3 Mann

Länge: 4,81 m

Breite: 2,22 m

Höhe: 1,99 m

Kampfgewicht: 8,9 t

Leistung: 140 PS

Höchstgeschwindigkeit: 39,5 km/h

Reichweite: 190 km (Straße), 126 km (Gelände)

Bewaffnung: 1 x 2-cm-KwK 30; 1 x 7,92-mm-MG 34

---

[295] Jentz, Thomas L.: Panzertruppen. The Complete Guide to the Creation & Combat Employment of Germany's Tank Force. 1933-1942. Schiffer Military History: Atglen, USA, 1996, p. 278.

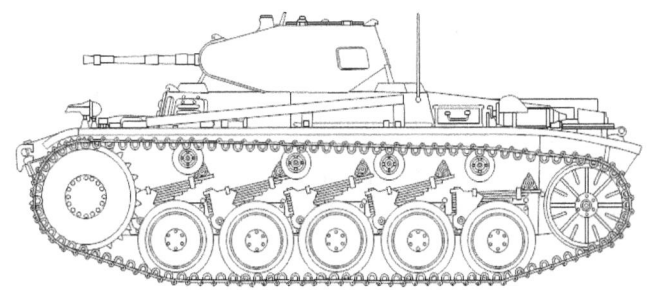

Panzerkampfwagen II Ausführung C

Technical data (Ausführung C)[296]

Crew: 3 men

Length: 4.81 m

Width: 2.22 m

Height: 1.99 m

Combat weight: 8.9 t

Power output: 140 hp

Maximum speed: 39.5 km/h

Range: 190 km (road), 126 km (terrain)

Armament: 1 x 2 cm KwK 30; 1 x 7.92 mm MG 34

---

[296] Jentz, Thomas L.: Panzertruppen. The Complete Guide to the Creation & Combat Employment of Germany's Tank Force. 1933-1942. Schiffer Military History: Atglen, USA, 1996, p. 278.

Panzerkampfwagen III

Der Panzerkampfwagen III hatte ursprünglich die Bezeichnung „Zugführerwagen". Der Entwicklungsauftrag wurde 1934 erteilt. 1936 gingen die ersten Panzer III in den Truppenversuch. Es folgten neue Varianten mit veränderten Laufwerken, Federungen und anderen Verbesserungen. Allerdings wurde erst 1939 die erste größere Serie der Ausführung E mit 100 Stück in Auftrag gegeben[297]. Zukunftsweisend bei diesem Panzer war, dass er über eine fünfköpfige Besatzung und moderne Funkausrüstung verfügte[298].

Der Panzer III war ursprünglich mit einer 3,7-cm Kanone und mehreren Maschinengewehren ausgerüstet. Allerdings wurde die Möglichkeit berücksichtigt den Panzer später mit einer stärkeren Waffe auszurüsten[299]. Im Laufe des Krieges fand dies auch mehrmals statt, so wurde die Bewaffnung zuerst auf eine mittlere 5-cm-Kanone und schließlich eine lange 5-cm-Kanone gesteigert. Als der Panzer III nicht mehr für die Bekämpfung von Panzer geeignet war, wurde er auf eine 7,5-cm-Kurzrohrkanone umgerüstet, die besser für die Bekämpfung von Infanterie und ungepanzerten Zielen geeignet war.

Zu Kriegsbeginn 1939 waren gerade einmal 3 % aller deutschen Panzer, die gegen Polen eingesetzt wurden Panzer III[300]. Beim Frankreichfeldzug Mai 1940 war dieser Anteil bereits auf 14 % gestiegen[301] und schließlich im Sommer 1941 zur Operation Barbarossa auf 29 % angewachsen. Damit war der Panzer III der häufigste deutsche Panzer für diese Operation[302].

---

[297] Hahn, Fritz: Waffen und Geheimwaffen des deutschen Heeres 1933-1945. Band 2: Panzer- und Sonderfahrzeuge, „Wunderwaffen", Verbrauch und Verluste. Dörfler Verlag: Eggolsheim, o. J., S. 31-32.

[298] Pöhlmann, Markus: Der Panzer und die Mechanisierung des Krieges: Eine deutsche Geschichte 1890 bis 1945. Ferdinand Schöningh: Paderborn, 2016, S. 269.

[299] Pöhlmann, Markus: Der Panzer und die Mechanisierung des Krieges: Eine deutsche Geschichte 1890 bis 1945. Ferdinand Schöningh: Paderborn, 2016, S. 269.

[300] Jentz, Thomas L.: Panzertruppen. The Complete Guide to the Creation & Combat Employment of Germany's Tank Force. 1933-1942. Schiffer Military History: Atglen, USA, 1996, p. 88.

[301] Frieser, Karl-Heinz: Blitzkrieg-Legende. Der Westfeldzug 1940. 4. Auflage. Oldenbourg Verlag: München, 2012, S. 44.

[302] Mueller-Hillebrand, Burkhart: Das deutsche Heer 1933-1945. Band II. E. S. Mittler & Sohn: Frankfurt am Main, 1956, S. 106.

Panzerkampfwagen III

The Panzerkampfwagen III originally had the designation "Platoon Leader Vehicle". The development order was placed in 1934. In 1936, the first Panzer III tanks were used during troop trials. New variants emerged with modified drives, suspensions and other improvements. However, it was not until 1939 that the first large production of 100 tanks (Ausf. E) was ordered[303]. A critical new feature of this tank was that it had a crew of five and modern radio equipment[304].

It was originally equipped with a 3.7 cm cannon and several machine guns, before it was considered to equip the tank later with a stronger weapon[305]. Throughout the course of the war the armament was changed several times, with the main upgrade being the installation of a was medium length and then a long 5 cm gun. When the Panzer III was no longer capable of fighting tanks, it was converted to carry a short barrel 7.5 cm cannon, which was better suited for fighting infantry and unarmored targets with high-explosive shells.

Only 3% of all German tanks used against Poland were Panzer III[306]. In May 1940 during the French campaign, this share had already risen to 14%[307] and finally increased to 29% in summer 1941 for Operation Barbarossa, making it the most common German tank for this operation[308].

---

[303] Hahn, Fritz: Waffen und Geheimwaffen des deutschen Heeres 1933-1945. Band 2: Panzer- und Sonderfahrzeuge, "Wunderwaffen", Verbrauch und Verluste. Dörfler Verlag: Eggolsheim, o. J., S. 31-32.

[304] Pöhlmann, Markus: Der Panzer und die Mechanisierung des Krieges: Eine deutsche Geschichte 1890 bis 1945. Ferdinand Schöningh: Paderborn, 2016, S. 269.

[305] Pöhlmann, Markus: Der Panzer und die Mechanisierung des Krieges: Eine deutsche Geschichte 1890 bis 1945. Ferdinand Schöningh: Paderborn, 2016, S. 269.

[306] Jentz, Thomas L.: Panzertruppen. The Complete Guide to the Creation & Combat Employment of Germany's Tank Force. 1933-1942. Schiffer Military History: Atglen, USA, 1996, p. 88.

[307] Frieser, Karl-Heinz: Blitzkrieg-Legende. Der Westfeldzug 1940. 4. Auflage. Oldenbourg Verlag: München, 2012, S. 44.

[308] Mueller-Hillebrand, Burkhart: Das deutsche Heer 1933-1945. Band II. E. S. Mittler & Sohn: Frankfurt am Main, 1956, S. 106.

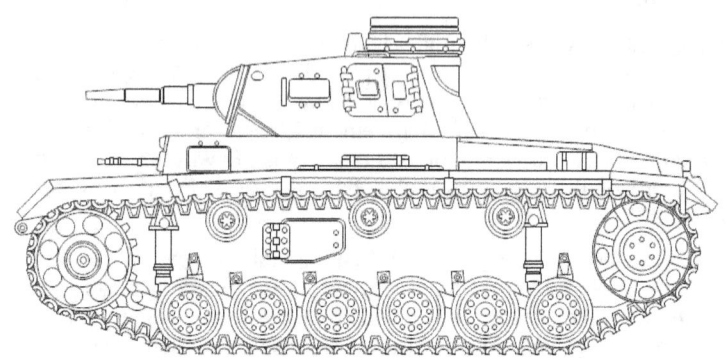

Panzerkampfwagen III Ausführung E

Technische Daten (Ausführung E)[309]

Besatzung: 5 Mann

Länge: 5,38 m

Breite: 2,91 m

Höhe: 2,44 m

Kampfgewicht: 19,5 t

Leistung: 265 PS

Höchstgeschwindigkeit: 67 km/h

Reichweite: 165 (Straße), 95 (Gelände)

Bewaffnung: 1 x 3,7-cm-KwK 36 L/46.5; 3 x 7,92-mm-MG34

---

[309] Jentz, Thomas L.: Panzertruppen. The Complete Guide to the Creation & Combat Employment of Germany's Tank Force. 1933-1942. Schiffer Military History: Atglen, USA, 1996, p. 279.

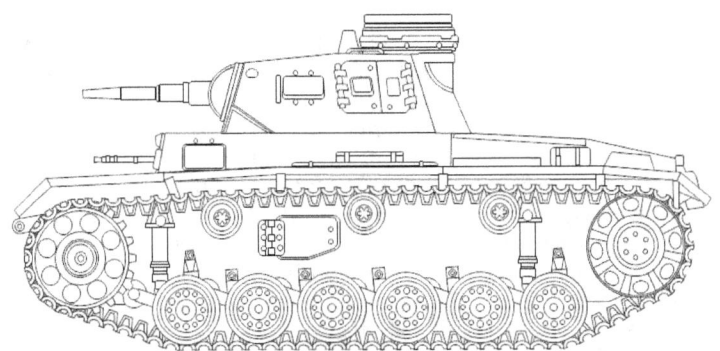

Panzerkampfwagen III Ausführung E

Technical data (Ausführung F)[310]

Crew: 5 men

Length: 5.38 m

width: 2.91 m

Height: 2.44 m

Combat weight: 19.5 t

Power output: 265 hp

Maximum speed: 67 km/h

Range: 165 (road), 95 (terrain)

Armament: 1 x 3.7 cm KwK 36 L/46.5; 3 x 7.92 mm MG 34

---

[310] Jentz, Thomas L.: Panzertruppen. The Complete Guide to the Creation & Combat Employment of Germany's Tank Force. 1933-1942. Schiffer Military History: Atglen, USA, 1996, p. 279.

Panzerkampfwagen IV

Der Panzerkampfwagen IV hatte ursprünglich die Bezeichnung „Begleitwagen". Er verfügte über eine starke Bewaffnung mit dem Kaliber von 7,5-cm, allerdings mit einem Kurzrohr. Diese Kurzrohr-Konfiguration hat zur Folge, dass die Mündungsgeschwindigkeit relativ gering ist und die Genauigkeit reduziert ist. Dementsprechend war diese Bewaffnung spätestens nach dem Auftreten von stark gepanzerten Panzern wie den sowjetischen T-34 und KW-1 nicht mehr für den Kampf gegen Panzer geeignet[311]. Die Produktion lief bereits 1936 an, allerdings kam es wie beim Panzer III zu mehreren Anpassungen. Deshalb war zu Kriegsbeginn nur eine geringe Anzahl von Panzer IV vorhanden. Genauso wie der Panzer III verfügte der Panzer IV über eine fünfköpfige Besatzung. Der relativ große Turmkranz und Rumpf erlaubte auch den Einbau einer größeren Waffe, und 1942 wurde der Panzer IV mit einer langen 7,5-cm-Kanone ausgestattet. Mit dieser Bewaffnung stellte der Panzer IV bis zu Kriegsende für die meisten alliierten Panzer eine Bedrohung dar. Der Panzer IV wurde damit auch zum „Arbeitspferd" der deutschen Panzerwaffe.

Zu Kriegsbeginn 1939 waren nur 7 % aller deutschen Panzer, die gegen Polen eingesetzt wurden Panzer IV[312]. Beim Frankreichfeldzug im Mai 1940 war dieser Anteil auf 11 % gestiegen,[313] im Sommer 1941 zur Operation Barbarossa jedoch kaum verändert auf lediglich 13 %[314].

---

[311] Pöhlmann, Markus: Der Panzer und die Mechanisierung des Krieges: Eine deutsche Geschichte 1890 bis 1945. Ferdinand Schöningh: Paderborn, 2016, S. 269-270. Vergleiche hierzu Punkt 170 in dieser H. Dv.

[312] Jentz, Thomas L.: Panzertruppen. The Complete Guide to the Creation & Combat Employment of Germany's Tank Force. 1933-1942. Schiffer Military History: Atglen, USA, 1996, p. 88.

[313] Frieser, Karl-Heinz: Blitzkrieg-Legende. Der Westfeldzug 1940. 4. Auflage. Oldenbourg Verlag: München, 2012, S. 44.

[314] Mueller-Hillebrand, Burkhart: Das deutsche Heer 1933-1945. Band II. E. S. Mittler & Sohn: Frankfurt am Main, 1956, S. 106.

Panzerkampfwagen IV

The Panzerkampfwagen IV was originally designated as "Accompanying Vehicle"[315]. It had a strong armament featuring a large caliber of 7.5 cm, but with a short barrel. This short barrel configuration results in a relatively low muzzle velocity and reduced accuracy. Once well-armored tanks like the Soviet T-34 and KV-1 were encountered this armament was not was not ideally suited for fighting tanks[316]. Although production commenced already in 1936, but like the Panzer III there were several adaptations. With the beginning of the war in September 1939 only a small number of these tanks were available. Just like Panzer III the Panzer IV had a crew of five. The relatively large turret ring and hull allowed the installation of a larger weapon and in 1942 Panzer IV was upgraded to use a long-barreled 7.5 cm gun. With this weapon it remained a threat to most Allied tanks until the end of the war. The Panzer IV thus became the "workhorse" of the German Armor Branch.

In Poland, only 7% of all German tanks used were Panzer IV[317]. During the French campaign in 1940 this share had risen to 11%[318] although it remained relatively stagnant as more than a year later for Operation Barbarossa it had only risen to 13%[319].

---

[315] The German "Begleitwagen" is a composite word, constructed out of "Begleitung" meaning "accompanying" and "Wagen" meaning "vehicle", "carriage" or "car". It could also be translated as an "escort vehicle" or "support vehicle".

[316] Pöhlmann, Markus: Der Panzer und die Mechanisierung des Krieges: Eine deutsche Geschichte 1890 bis 1945. Ferdinand Schöningh: Paderborn, 2016, S. 269-270. Compare this to Number 171 in this regulation.

[317] Jentz, Thomas L.: Panzertruppen. The Complete Guide to the Creation & Combat Employment of Germany's Tank Force. 1933-1942. Schiffer Military History: Atglen, USA, 1996, p. 88.

[318] Frieser, Karl-Heinz: Blitzkrieg-Legende. Der Westfeldzug 1940. 4. Auflage. Oldenbourg Verlag: München, 2012, S. 44.

[319] Mueller-Hillebrand, Burkhart: Das deutsche Heer 1933-1945. Band II. E. S. Mittler & Sohn: Frankfurt am Main, 1956, S. 106.

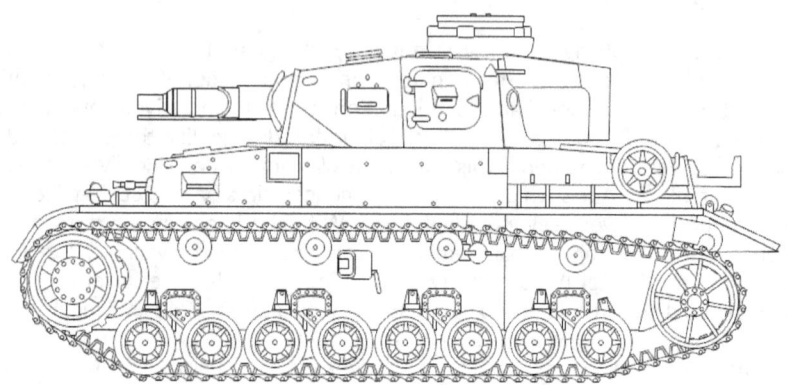

Panzerkampfwagen IV – Ausführung E

Technische Daten (Ausführung E)[320]

Besatzung: 5 Mann

Länge: 5,92 m

Breite: 2,83 m

Höhe: 2,68 m

Kampfgewicht: 22 t

Leistung: 265 PS

Höchstgeschwindigkeit: 42 km/h

Reichweite: 210 (Straße), 130 (Gelände)

Bewaffnung: 1 x 7,5-cm-KwK 37 L/24; 2 x 7,92-mm-MG34

---

[320] Jentz, Thomas L.: Panzertruppen. The Complete Guide to the Creation & Combat Employment of Germany's Tank Force. 1933-1942. Schiffer Military History: Atglen, USA, 1996, p. 280.

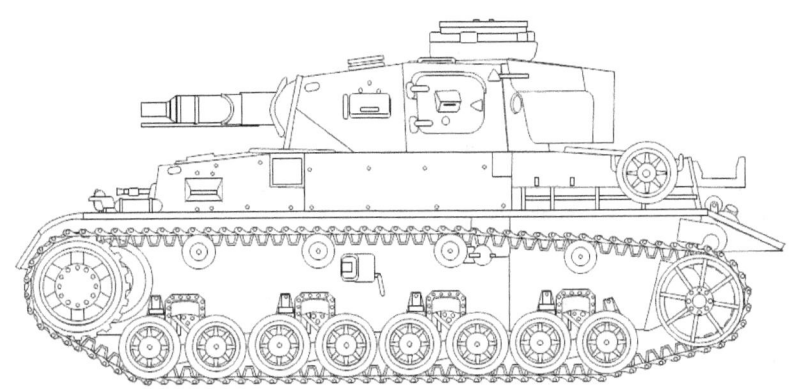

Panzerkampfwagen IV – Ausführung E

Technical data (Ausführung E)[321]

Crew: 5 men

Length: 5.92 m

Width: 2.83 m

Height: 2.68 m

Combat weight: 22 t

Power output: 265 hp

Maximum speed: 42 km/h

Range: 210 (road), 130 (terrain)

Armament: 1 x 7.5 cm KwK 37 L/24; 2 x 7.92 mm MG 34

---

[321] Jentz, Thomas L.: Panzertruppen. The Complete Guide to the Creation & Combat Employment of Germany's Tank Force. 1933-1942. Schiffer Military History: Atglen, USA, 1996, p. 280.

Bibliographie / Bibliography

Quellen / Primary Sources

BArch, RH 1/365: H. Dv. 1a: Verzeichnis der planmäßigen Heeres-Druckvorschriften, Januar 1942.

BArch, RH 1/366: Anhang 1 zur H. Dv. 1a Verzeichnis der von AHA/HDv verwalteten außerplanmäßigen Heeres-Vorschriften(D-Vorschriften), 1.6.1941, 1941 – 1943.

BArch, RH 1/384: H. Dv. 1/8: Kriegssoll (Heer) an Vorschriften (K. a. V.).- Heft 8: Panzertruppe – Feldheer, Oktober 1943.

BArch, RH 1/1881: H. Dv. 470/22a: Ausbildungsvorschrift für die schnellen Truppen.- Heft 22a: Schulschießübungen von Panzerkampfwagen II, August 1942.

BArch, RH 8/5909: D 1/1+: Verzeichnis der geheimen außerplanmäßigen Heeres-Vorschriften (D+), 1.3.1937, 1937 – 1939.

BArch, RH 8/5910: D 1/1+: Verzeichnis der geheimen außerplanmäßigen Heeres-Vorschriften (D+), 1.2.1939.

BArch, RH 8/5912: Verzeichnis der waffentechnischen D+-Vorschriften, Oktober 1941.

BArch, RH 11-I/83: Merkblatt 25a/16: Vorläufiges Merkblatt „Der M.P.-Zug der Grenadier-Kompanie", 1.2.1944.

Bieringer: Nachschubfibel. Zweite verbesserte Auflage. Verlag „Offene Worte", Berlin, Germany, 1938.

Bundesministerium der Verteidigung: Katalog der Druckvorschriften der ehemaligen deutschen Wehrmacht – Teil 1 Heer, Bonn, 1960, S. 119.

FM 7-5: Infantry Field Manual: Organization and Tactics of Infantry – The Rifle Battalions, War Department: Washington, USA, 1940.

FM 17-10: Armored Force Field Manual: Tactics and Technique. War Department: Washington, USA, March, 1942.

FM 17-32: Armored Force Field Manual: The Tank Company, Light and Medium. War Department: Washington, USA, August, 1942.

FM 17-15: Tank Platoon. Headquarters of the Army, USA, April, 1996.

Gesterding, Schwatlo; Feyerabend: Unteroffizierthemen. Fünfte, neubearbeite Auflage. E. S. Mittler & Sohn: Berlin, Germany, 1938.

Haas, Walter: Soldatenlexikon. Ein Merkbuch für den Infanteriedienst. Franckh'sche Verlagshandlung: Stuttgart, Germany, o.J.

H. Dv. 130/2a: Ausbildungsvorschrift für die Infanterie. Heft 2a. Die Schützenkompanie. Verlag „Offene Worte", Berlin, Germany, 16. März 1941.

H. Dv. 300/1: Truppenführung (T.F.) I. Teil. E. S. Mittler & Sohn: Berlin, Germany, 1936 (17. Oktober 1933).

H. Dv. 470/1: Ausbildungsvorschrift für die Panzertruppe. Heft 1. Verlage „Offene Worte", Berlin, Germany, 2. Oktober 1938.

H. Dv. 470/5b: Ausbildungsvorschrift für die Panzertruppe. Heft 5b. Die Ausbildung am Panzerkampfwagen II (2 cm) Sonderkraftfahrzeug 121 (Sd. Kfz. 121), 1939.

H. Dv. 470/6: Ausbildungsvorschrift für die Panzertruppe. Heft 6: Die leichte Panzerkompanie. Ernst Siegfried Mittler und Sohn, Berlin, Germany, 2. September 1940.

H. Dv. 470/7: Ausbildungsvorschrift für die Panzertruppe. Heft 7: Die mittlere Panzerkompanie. Reichsdruckerei, Berlin, Germany, 1. Mai 1941.

Kühlwein, Fritz: Die Gruppe im Gefecht. (Die neue Gruppe). E. S. Mittler & Sohn: Berlin, Germany, 1940.

TM 30-506: German Military Dictionary, War Department: Washington, USA, May, 1944.

TsAMO, F 500, Op. 12480, D 137: Nachrichtenblatt der Panzertruppen. Nr. 1, 15. Juli 1943.

Literatur / Secondary Sources

Condell, Bruce (ed.); Zabecki, David T. (ed.): On the German Art of War. Truppenführung. Stackpole Books: Mechanicsburg, PA, USA, 2009 (2001).

Frieser, Karl-Heinz: Blitzkrieg-Legende. Der Westfeldzug 1940. 4. Auflage. Oldenbourg Verlag: München, Germany, 2012.

Glantz, David et al.: Slaughterhouse: The Encyclopedia of the Eastern Front. Military Book Club: USA, 2002.

Hahn, Fritz: Waffen und Geheimwaffen des deutschen Heeres 1933-1945. Band 2: Panzer- und Sonderfahrzeuge, „Wunderwaffen", Verbrauch und Verluste. Dörfler Verlag: Eggolsheim, Germany, ohne Jahr.

Jentz, Thomas L.: Panzertruppen. The Complete Guide to the Creation & Combat Employment of Germany's Tank Force. 1933-1942. Schiffer Military History: Atglen, USA, 1996.

Keilig, Wolf: Das deutsche Heer 1939-1945. Podzun-Verlag: Bad Nauheim, Germany, ohne Jahr.

Mueller-Hillebrand, Burkhart: Das deutsche Heer 1933-1945. Band II. E. S. Mittler & Sohn: Frankfurt am Main, Germany, 1956.

Niehorster, Leo W.G.: German World War II Organizational Series. Volume 1/I: Mechanized Army Divisions and Waffen-SS Units (1.09.1939). The Military Press: Buckinghamshire, UK, 2007 (2004).

Niehorster, Leo W.G., German World War II Organizational Series. Volume 3/I: Mechanized Army Divisions and Waffen-SS Units (22 June 1941), Milton Keynes, 2007.

Pöhlmann, Markus: Der Panzer und die Mechanisierung des Krieges: Eine deutsche Geschichte 1890 bis 1945. Ferdinand Schöningh: Paderborn, Germany, 2016.

Schneider, Wolfgang: Panzer Tactics. German Small-Unit Armor Tactics in World War II. Stackpole Books: Mechanicsburg, PA, USA, 2005.

Schramm, Percy E. (Hrsg.): Kriegstagebuch des OKW. Eine Dokumentation: 1942. Band 4. Teilband 2. Bechtermünz: Augsburg, Germany, 2005.

Stahel, David: Operation Barbarossa and Germany's Defeat in the East. Cambridge University Press: Cambridge, UK, 2011 (2009).

Also by

Military History Group
Footnotes or bust!

STURMZUG
Tactics of the German Assault Platoon 44

STURMZUG – Tactics of the German Assault Platoon 44
Bernhard Kast and Christoph Bergs

STURMZUG – Tactics of the German Assault Platoon 44 is a must-read for anyone interested in World War 2 combat and tactics. Centered around the assault platoon equipped with the iconic Sturmgewehr 44, the documents included in this book include never before published information on Wehrmacht infantry tactics.

This book includes the original tactics for the attack, the defense, retreat, firefight and the assault with hand grenades by the Assault Platoon. Carefully recreated illustrations of the original documents provide easy to read visual representations of firing stances, unit formations and maps. Together with supplementary information drawn from German pamphlets and regulations, this provides a rich comprehension of German unit-based tactics straight from the original documents.

Presenting a side-by-side German-English translation, this book was carefully edited to remain true to the original documents in both content and layout.

Available at: http://sturmzug.com

STUKA
The Doctrine of the German Dive Bomber

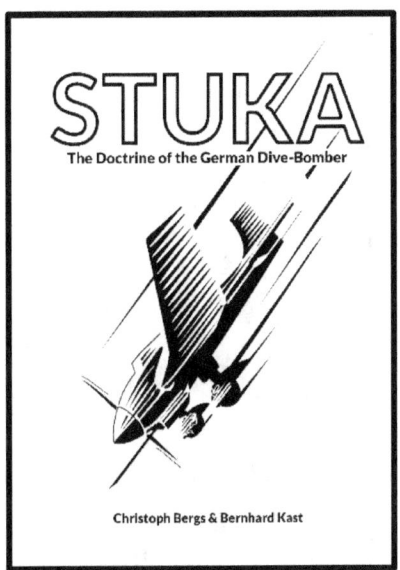

STUKA - The Doctrine of the German Dive-Bomber
Christoph Bergs and Bernhard Kast

STUKA - The Doctrine of the German Dive-Bomber includes more than a dozen original Luftwaffe documents translated into English, alongside introductory essays that provide additional information and context. These documents have been carefully curated and gathered from various archives to provide you with the best foundation on the tactics, doctrine, organization, training and operational experience with the Junkers Ju 87 dive-bomber.

Inside Stuka - The Doctrine of the German Dive-Bomber you will find:
- A full organizational breakdown of a Sturzkampfgeschwader,
- the training manual on how to dive-bomb with the Junkers Ju 87,
- the tasks and roles of dive-bombers in the Luftwaffe,
- reports from operations in Poland, the Soviet Union and Crete,
- technical information and references,

as well as numerous essays on the Junkers Ju 87, its production, legacy and operation during the Second World War.

Available at: http://stukabook.com

IS-2
Development, Design and Production of Stalin's Warhammer

IS-2 – Development, Design and Production of Stalin's Warhammer
Peter Samsonov

The IS-2 is the quintessential Soviet heavy tank from World War 2. Heavily armored and boasting a fearsome 122mm gun, this tank matched the German panzers on the Eastern front by more than just its fierce appearance. This tank's history is told from the beginning of the Soviet heavy tank programme until the very end of World War 2, in the most detailed and complete account of its development, design and production available in English.

Supported by extensive research of Russian language sources, this publication includes a comprehensive breakdown of prototypes, the Soviet analysis of weaknesses in German tanks including the Tiger and Panther, the development of the 122mm gun, the principles of the new tank's armor layout and a wealth of technical data.

Available at: http://is-2-tank.com/

www.ingramcontent.com/pod-product-compliance
Lightning Source LLC
Chambersburg PA
CBHW060557230426
43670CB00011B/1865